BEING PREGNAN

the woman's answer book

BEING PREGNANT

Ruth Steinberg & Linda Robinson

ANAYA PUBLISHERS
LONDON

First published in Great Britain in 1989
by Anaya Publishers Ltd, 49 Neal Street, London WC2H 9PJ

Editor: Nancy Duin
Designer: Susie Home
Illustrator: Sharon Penks

British Library Cataloguing in Publication Data
A CIP catalogue record for ths book is available from the British Library.

ISBN 1-85470-003-0

Typeset by Keyspools
Printed and bound in Great Britain by Redwood Burn

Contents

CONTENTS

INTRODUCTION

Only in relatively recent years have women had a choice about whether to become pregnant or not. It was an accepted as well as expected part of a woman's life that she would marry and start a family. However, women were given very little information about having a baby. If they were lucky, they learned from watching their mothers and aunts experience the miracle, but often it was a strange and frightening event over which they had no control.

Because the activities of daily living took so much of a woman's energy, she rarely had time to focus on what was happening within her. The event simply occurred. Without her knowing *how* it happened, her body formed and produced another human being.

A woman's body has been designed especially for reproduction. In an amazingly complex system of hormonal factors, an egg matures, becomes fertilized, implants, and develops into a foetus. At the same time, the body prepares itself to have a baby. All this happens without the consent, and beyond the control, of the woman.

Aside from all the social and emotional factors involved in childbearing today, the event is a natural, normal biological means of preserving the species. Pregnancy should not be looked upon as an illness or a handicap, but as a healthy, wholesome process. It is a natural part of womanhood.

PART I

Preparing for Change

CHAPTER ONE

Finding Out You Are Pregnant

If you have been trying to conceive, chances are you will be looking and waiting for any sign that you could be pregnant. Once you have decided to start a family and your period is a few days late, the chorus begins to ring through your head: "I wonder if I'm pregnant, I wonder if this is it." Every stomach symptom is perceived as morning sickness until either your period starts or enough time has elapsed that you now *know* that you are pregnant. The majority of women do not need a pregnancy test to tell them that they are pregnant; most of the time, they just know. It is described as a feeling. It's not an ache or a pain or a stomach upset . . . just a feeling. The reaction to this feeling may range from jubilation to despair, depending on whether or not the pregnancy was planned.

Some women say that they could tell they were pregnant as soon as they conceived, and for those who are very much in tune with their bodies, this may be the case. The telling sign for most women, however, is a missed period. Occasionally a woman may have a small amount of bleeding at the time the egg is implanting in the uterus. This is called "implantation bleeding", and since it happens ten days to two weeks after conception, it may be mistaken for a light period. There are usually no detrimental effects from this, except to confuse the due date. Be sure to tell your doctor or midwife if your last period was in any way unusual for you.

Pregnancy tests

It used to be that a pregnancy was confirmed when the woman felt the baby move. Now a pregnancy can be diagnosed much earlier.

Home pregnancy tests are becoming increasingly popular and more reliable. One of the advantages of these tests is the privacy they provide. No medical person need be involved; you can simply go to a chemist, purchase the test and follow the directions. The main disadvantages are that they are slightly less accurate than a lab test, and you have to pay for them. In addition, you should wait until your period is at least one week overdue. Some women are not comfortable with the mechanics of a home pregnancy test; they prefer to have someone else perform the test for them.

An alternative to a home pregnancy test is a urine test done either at a hospital laboratory, or at your doctor's surgery. You must provide the urine sample (usually one taken when you urinate first thing in the morning). For an accurate result, you should wait until your period is at least five days overdue. Some labs do not give the results directly to the patient, although the results are immediately available. In that case, you must contact your doctor for the results, which takes additional time.

Blood tests are also available to diagnose a pregnancy. These tests must be done in a laboratory, and there is a small amount of pain involved in this procedure. However, the results of a blood test are much more accurate than a urine test. Also, the diagnosis may be made two days after a missed period.

Pregnancy tests can sometimes give false results. Most of the time these are "false negative" results (the test says you are not pregnant when you really are), and they occur most frequently with the urine test. Having the test done too early is a common reason for receiving a false negative result. Often you (or your partner) is so anxious to know for sure if you are pregnant, it is difficult to wait until your period is a full week or two late. If the urine is very dilute, such as a sample taken late in the afternoon after consuming large amounts of fluid, the result may also be falsely negative. To avoid this, the first morning urine should be used for the test.

When is your baby due?

The duration of a full-term pregnancy is calculated as 38–40 weeks from the first day of your last period. This calculation can be confusing – after all, most women will not ovulate and conceive until two weeks *after* their last normal period. However, the time period of

38–40 weeks takes this two-week gap into account. Once the time of your last period has been established, you will be given a "due date" – that is, the date by which your baby is expected to be born. However, babies are quite well known for *not* arriving when expected. It is a good idea to be ready for the birth at any time during the two weeks before and two weeks after the "due date". If your periods are irregular, or if your last period was abnormal for you, an ultrasound scan (*see* p. 67) in the first half of the pregnancy will help establish the due date.

Doctors and midwives always refer to pregnancies in weeks. This is because, historically, pregnancy is based on lunar months. A lunar month consists of exactly four weeks as opposed to calendar months, which may vary in length. The milestones of pregnancy are also more easily documented when using weeks. For instance, morning sickness usually ends at about 12 weeks, you usually feel the baby move at 18–20 weeks, the heartbeat can be heard with a special device at 12 weeks and with a foetoscope at 16–20 weeks.

The following chart gives a comparison of months and weeks:

Month completed	Weeks
1	6
2	$10\frac{1}{2}$
3	15
4	$19\frac{1}{2}$
5	$23\frac{1}{2}$
6	28
7	32
8	$36\frac{1}{2}$
9	40

Antenatal care and the place of birth

When you have established that you are pregnant, you must decide where and from whom you want to receive care during your pregnancy ("antenatal care"), and where you want your baby to be born.

Most women first go to their family doctor. He or she may then take on the responsibility for your antenatal care or may refer you to an antenatal unit at a local hospital. Alternatively, you can contact a hospital direct; you do not need a letter of referral from your doctor.

If you are considering a hospital, ask other women in your area about their experiences. Some hospitals are more popular than others, so it is a good idea to book as early as possible. Hospital antenatal clinics can sometimes seem like conveyor belts, with long periods of waiting and different personnel at every visit. However, in recent years, some clinics have tried to avoid these problems, and in any case, you may want to become as familiar as possible with the hospital in which your baby will be born.

You may prefer to have your antenatal care from your own doctor and the community midwife attached to his or her surgery. However, you may have to attend a hospital antenatal clinic for a few tests.

You also have a number of choices about where your baby will be born and who should attend you during the birth.

Hospital

The majority of women today have their babies in hospital. Here, qualified staff and up-to-date equipment are all at hand in case of emergency. If the birth is uncomplicated, you will be attended by a midwife; if assistance is needed, there is always a doctor nearby to help, and the consultant obstetrician in charge can always be contacted if needed. However, it is unlikely that any of these people will be the same as those who have cared for you in the antenatal clinic. To try to make themselves less impersonal to expectant mothers (and their partners), many hospitals run antenatal classes (exercises and parentcraft) and may have tours of the labour ward and delivery rooms.

GP Units

In some areas, you can opt for care from your general practitioner and midwife both for antenatal care and for the actual birth. Antenatal care would be carried out at your doctor's surgery, and your baby would then be born at a "GP unit", staffed by midwives and GPs trained in obstetrics. These are either separate small hospitals or are attached to larger hospitals. This continuity of care has much to recommend it.

The "Domino" scheme

Another choice is the "Domino" scheme. "Domino" stands for "DOMiciliary IN and Out". In this case, your GP and midwife take care of you during your pregnancy; then, when you begin labour, your midwife comes to your home and takes you to hospital to deliver your baby. Your GP and the hospital staff only become involved if needed. If everything goes well, you can return home in a few hours, and your midwife will continue caring for you and your baby.

Home birth

Finally, you could choose to have a home birth. Many women prefer this, finding that they can be more relaxed and "natural" in their own familiar surroundings, and some prefer to involve the whole family in the birth, something that can be quite difficult to achieve in hospital.

For the most part, home births are just as safe as hospital births. However, there may be good reasons why a home delivery would be unsuitable for you and/or your baby – for instance, you may be having twins, you may have had a difficult labour in the past, you may have a medical condition that would make it dangerous for you and your baby to be too far from the emergency equipment found in a hospital. If those caring for you recommend that you do not have a home birth, you should seriously consider what they say. However, it has to be said that there is still great prejudice against home births among many members of the medical profession, and you may find that this is the reason why home birth is not recommended. Nevertheless, you are entitled by law to have your baby at home if you want to, and a midwife must be provided.

Other considerations

Whatever type of care you opt for, there are a number of questions that you could ask to make sure that your antenatal care and the birth are what *you* want them to be.

For example, you may be keen to have as "natural" a childbirth as possible. In this case, ask if you will be able to move around as much as you want to during labour or does the hospital have a policy of continuously monitoring the foetal heartbeat and contractions, in which case you may have to stay in bed. What sorts of pain medication will be offered, and would it be possible to avoid using any at all? You may want to ask if you will be able to adopt any position – such as squatting or getting on all fours – during the actual birth or is it hospital policy for all women in labour to lie on their backs. Are all women given episiotomies (*see* p. 147) or do hospital staff wait to see if they are needed?

17

Who is with you during your labour and the birth can also be important. Does the hospital just allow partners or can you bring a friend or family member?

What happens after the birth can be equally important. Can your partner stay with you right after the birth? Do babies stay with their mothers all the time or are they put in a nursery at night? Is breast-feeding encouraged? Can your other children visit you in hospital? Can your partner be with you at times other than during visiting hours?

Some of these things matter more to some women than to others. Think carefully about what you want, and ask those who will be caring for you. Remember that medical staff should be your advocates, not your enemies. Let your desires be known, but be open to the information and expertise they have to offer. If you are not sure that everything will be to your satisfaction, you can try to persuade them to do things your way. If this does not work, you can try to go elsewhere or, if this is impossible, make the best of what you can get. However, most women are very pleased with the care they receive during labour and childbirth, and an increasing number of hospitals are modifying their procedures to make childbirth the special, intimate occasion that it can ideally be. (*See also* "Developing a birth plan" on p. 152.)

CHAPTER TWO

The Changes of Pregnancy

A baby introduces major lifestyle changes which can take some getting used to. Early on in the pregnancy, you may begin to think about those impending changes, and it is normal to feel a certain sense of grief and loss no matter how planned and wanted the pregnancy is. The loss of freedom that comes with the birth of a child is what most women feel strongly about. Once your baby is born, it won't be as easy to pick up and do things on the spur of the moment if that has been your style. You no longer will have just yourself to get ready: having a baby in the house requires more planning and creates more constraints than in a childless household. Even though this may eventually become an accepted, cherished way of life, when first confronted with the thought you may say, "Uh oh. How am I going to handle that?" Be assured that those feelings are normal. It's even common to resent the baby a little as you make the mental adjustment. No need to feel guilty. All normal.

Emotional adjustment

When a pregnancy is unplanned, the period of adjustment may take longer and be more difficult. The sense of the loss of freedom and the sacrifice of future plans can be overwhelming. Depending on whom you have to give you support (both emotional and financial) and your ability to talk about your worries, the adjustment may take anywhere from two weeks to four months to nine months. All this may be complicated by having to decide whether or not to terminate your pregnancy. If you decide against it, you may continue to wonder and worry about whether you have done the right thing.

Once you become pregnant, it may seem as if your hormones have gone crazy and you are at a loss when trying to cope with your emotions. Your partner may even feel that a "stranger" has invaded your body. The pregnancy hormones oestrogen and progesterone have a multitude of effects on the body, and play a part in the mood swings that are common very early in the pregnancy. Women tend to become more self-centred, focusing intently on the changes that are occurring within their bodies. It is common to become more irritable, impatient and intolerant of minor annoyances which you used to deal with quite easily. You may also tend to cry a lot. It may be some consolation to know that, again, this is all normal. At about 14 weeks, the mood swings diminish, but all through the pregnancy you may tend to be more emotional.

You have little control over the changes that your body is going through, so you should take advantage of those changes over which you do have control. Try to acquire a maternity wardrobe that you feel is attractive. Maternity clothes can be very expensive, and the cost of new ones may be prohibitive. However, many women borrow clothes from friends and relatives, and because these clothes are worn for relatively short periods of time, they usually survive several pregnancies. Try to find colours that flatter you. Fortunately, in recent years the designers of maternity clothes have become a little more creative and there are more styles to choose from. In addition, some kinds of non-maternity clothes are naturally oversized. This allows you to purchase clothing that is in style, fits you for a good part of the pregnancy, and can be worn after your baby is born. Don't underestimate how important attractive clothing is. It helps you to have a much more positive body image.

Bodily changes: what to expect month by month

In addition to the emotional changes brought on by pregnancy, the physical changes required to create and nourish this new life are enormous. You'll want to know what's going on inside your body as this new person is forming. Every day this new being is changing and growing. And every day your body will change and you will feel different.

The first six weeks of pregnancy
The baby

Approximately two weeks after your last period, one of your ovaries releases a ripe egg (*ovum*) into one of the two Fallopian tubes. Fertilization occurs soon after the egg enters the tube, where it is surrounded by many sperm. Only one sperm penetrates the egg's coating and fuses with it. At this moment, the two cells join and become one. This new single cell, the product of the sperm from the father and the egg from the mother, contains all the information necessary to grow into a new human being.

From now until the 11th week of pregnancy, the baby is called an *embryo*. This is the time when all the organs and other parts of the body are formed. From the 11th week until the time of delivery, the baby is known as a *foetus*, when the body grows and develops so that it can sustain life outside the womb.

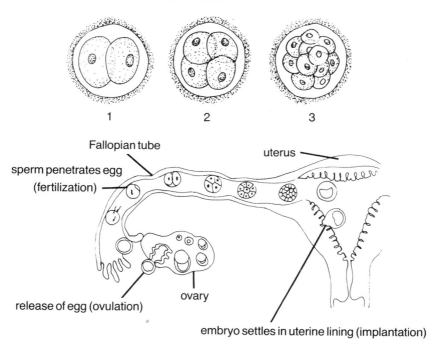

After the egg is fertilized by the sperm, it begins to divide, first into two cells (1), then four (2), then eight (3), continuing to do so until, after about three days, a hollow ball of 48 cells – called the blastocyst – enters the uterus, where it eventually implants in the lining.

The sex of the baby is determined at the moment of fertilization, and it is determined by whether the sperm contains an X or a Y chromosome. Chromosomes are microscopic structures that contain genes, which are the method by which information about growth and all aspects of our bodies are passed from one generation to another. The mother's egg always contains an X chromosome, but the father's sperm may contain an X chromosome or a Y chromosome. If an X-carrying sperm fertilizes the egg, a baby girl will develop. If a Y-carrying sperm fertilizes the egg, a baby boy will develop. So it is the father, not the mother, who determines whether the baby will be a boy or a girl.

About one hour after the sperm and egg fuse, the new cell begins to divide, from one cell to two, and from two cells to four, and from four cells to eight, as it travels down the tube towards the uterus (womb). By the third day after fertilization, a hollow ball of 48 cells enters the uterus. Over the next week, the expanding mass of cells mixes with the fluid within the uterus and settles in the lush bed of the uterine lining. At this point, cells destined for the baby and for the placenta begin to differentiate from one another.

The placenta (also known as the afterbirth) is a very important structure. It is the filter that brings food and oxygen to the baby and that carries away the baby's wastes. It is formed when the embryo settles into the uterine lining and sends out tiny finger-like projections – buds of circulation (*villi*) – from the baby to the mother. The two blood circulations remain separate, although they grow as close together as possible. This allows the placenta to separate from the mother's womb at the end of the pregnancy after the baby is delivered.

During the week that follows the implantation of the embryo in the uterine wall, there is both rapid growth of the circulation that develops between the mother and the baby, and rapid differentiation of the cell layers that will form your baby's different organs. In addition, a sac of fluid begins to form around the developing embryo. This "bag of water" will cushion the growing baby from shock and abrupt motion. At this point, the ball of cells which will become your baby will be about the size of the head of a pin.

The embryonic period is one of rapid growth and development. It is during this time that the baby's organs form. Therefore, it is now that the embryo is most susceptible to the harmful effects of drugs and other environmental agents (see Chapter 8). By the end of the third week of life, the embryo shows the beginnings of the nervous system and the formation of the heart tube. And by the end of the first month of life, the heart has begun to beat, the arm and leg buds have formed, and an indentation at the sites of the future eyes and ears can be detected. At this point, the embryo itself measures almost $\frac{1}{4}$ inch (6.5 mm) and assumes a recognizable prawn-like shape.

The baby

The embryo develops tremendously during its fifth and sixth weeks of life. (Remember, this will be the seventh and eighth week of your pregnancy, or seven to eight weeks since your last period.) During its fifth week, the beginnings of facial features develop. A slit-like opening – the primitive mouth – forms, connected to two small holes (the nasal pits, the primitive openings of the nose). The area of the eyes and their distinctive parts begin to emerge. The ends of the arms emerge as paddle-like structures called "hand plates". And the more advanced parts of the brain begin to form. At the end of the fifth week, the embryo is almost $\frac{3}{8}$ inch (1 cm) long.

As this rapidly forming being enters its sixth week of life, the cavities of the nose and mouth are more clearly delineated, but they are still a single connected structure. By the middle of that week, the upper lip forms, separating the nasal openings from the mouth. At the same time, paddle-like structures form at the end of the legs (the "foot plates"). By the end of the sixth week, the embryo is almost $\frac{1}{2}$ inch (1.2 cm) long, and has the beginnings of an identifiable ear structure, as well as a recognizable developing eye. The arms are bent at the elbows, a distinct wrist can be identified and webbed fingers can be discerned. Notches in the foot plate clearly identify the forming toes. Inside the baby, the circulatory, respiratory and digestive systems are rapidly developing.

The mother

You will now be six weeks from your last period. You will be feeling different. What can you expect?

At the end of the baby's second week of life, you will have just missed your period and you may have felt the first signs of pregnancy (nausea, breast tenderness, bloating, etc.) During the next four weeks, it is common to feel unusually fatigued; you may need to rest more. This is normal. You are creating a whole new human being and its support system, the placenta, and this requires a great deal of energy. If you need more rest, try to make time for it. If your usual amount of exercise tires you out, then cut back. If you are already taking care of another child, try to arrange for more help from your partner, your family, friends or neighbours. If friends or family have made offers to help with house chores and shopping, accept them gladly. By the 12th week of your pregnancy, the placenta will be well established and the feelings of fatigue will probably begin to recede. However, those feelings will probably return in the last weeks of the pregnancy, when you may need to arrange for help. Don't feel guilty; most people who have offered to help are only too glad to be of assistance.

Another common symptom of early pregnancy is "morning sickness". This refers to the nausea and, sometimes, vomiting which most commonly occurs in the morning but which may occur any time of day. This may also be accompanied by excessive salivation (*hyperptylism*). Although some women are lucky enough to escape these unpleasant symptoms, more than two-thirds of pregnant women will suffer to some degree. The cause of this nausea is not truly understood; however, anxiety is thought to exaggerate the severity of the problem. Is "morning sickness" dangerous? Will your baby get enough nutrients to grow and thrive? Except in unusual and extraordinarily severe cases (called *hyperemesis gravidarum*) your baby is protected. All available nutrients will go first to the baby before they are used by your body, and as a result, the baby will be adequately nourished. Generally, these symptoms will pass by the beginning of the third month.

Other common symptoms include heartburn and indigestion. These symptoms are probably caused by the increase in the hormone progesterone associated with pregnancy. Progesterone slows the emptying of the stomach and also allows the back-up of stomach acid into the oesophagus (gullet), which causes the symptom of heartburn. All of the unpleasant digestive symptoms of pregnancy may be alleviated by eating many, small, low-fat snacks instead of three large meals a day.

Almost all women complain of breast tenderness and fullness and tingling around the nipples. These changes are caused by the increased levels of oestrogen and progesterone throughout pregnancy. You may also notice that the pigmented area (the areola) around the nipple darkens. This is caused by another hormone whose level goes up in pregnancy. The breast tenderness and extreme sensitivity usually recede by the 12th week, but the breasts will increase in size by several bra sizes throughout pregnancy. You may have to wear bras of a number of different sizes as your pregnancy progresses. A good support bra will maintain breast tone and help alleviate upper back pain that can result from the muscles there having to support larger breasts. After the baby is born, the breasts will return to their more usual size. The darkening around the nipples will very slightly diminish but it will remain darker than it was before pregnancy.

Many women feel the urge to urinate more frequently. The cause for this symptom is not fully understood since there are women with perfectly healthy pregnancies who urinate with their usual frequency. Later on in pregnancy, most women will complain of urinary frequency because the baby's well-developed head (or bottom) presses against the bladder.

Weeks 7–10
The baby
By the end of the tenth week of pregnancy (ten weeks from your last period) the embryo will have fully developed its basic parts and internal organs.

During the ninth and tenth weeks of pregnancy, it will take on a distinctly human appearance. The eyelids will begin to form, separate fingers and toes are easily recognized, the body begins to elongate, strong bone starts to replace the flexible cartilage that had earlier been laid down, and the external genitals begin to differentiate into male or female. The baby, now called a *foetus*, measures $1\frac{1}{2}$ inches (3.8 cm) in length from head to bottom. The head will be comparatively large, being almost equal to the size of the rest of the body.

The embryo at 10 weeks: this is its actual size in the womb. It has many human features, and weighs about ¼ oz (8 g). From now on, this new life is known as a foetus.

25

The mother

You will now be in the middle of your third month of pregnancy. How will you feel? Many of the earlier symptoms of nausea, heartburn and indigestion may persist. You may become flushed and notice that your heart is beating more rapidly. These symptoms are caused by the necessary increase in blood flow and blood volume that your body has to produce in order to support the pregnancy. You may become more aware of the prominent blue or dark veins which first appear on your breasts and which can then be seen on your abdomen, thighs and buttocks. These also are a result of the increased blood flow as well as of the hormonal effects on the skin and the increased fluid retained by the skin which allow the veins under the skin to appear more noticeable.

Emotionally, you may feel very fragile, weepy, irritable and moody. You may cry easily and with seemingly no provocation. You may find that you can't sort out your emotions, that sadness and joy, anxiety and unbounded elation are all jumbled together. Don't panic. The enormous outpouring of hormones that are required to sustain a pregnancy can also send you on an irrational and unpredictable roller-coaster. Ask for emotional support from your partner and your friends. You may even want to seek out support groups or professional counselling – but medication is almost never required. As you complete your third month, you will have survived the first one-third – known as the first *trimester* – of your pregnancy.

Weeks 11–12

The baby

The foetus will measure about 3 inches (7.5 cm) from head to buttocks and will weigh about 1 ounce (30 g). The growth of the body has accelerated so that the head will become less disproportionately large. The foetus will now have a face which appears human, with a recognizable profile featuring the recently formed chin. The eyes, ears and tooth roots are basically formed. The foetus will have skin and nails, but not yet any hair. All of the body systems will now be formed, urine will begin to be produced, and the external genitals will begin visibly to take on the characteristics of either male or female. The baby will usually begin to move at 12 weeks, even though you will not be able to feel it. And by this time, the placenta will be well formed and fully functioning.

The uterus will have increased in size so that it now appears just over the pubic bone. Your doctor or midwife will be able to hear the foetal heart with an ultrasonic device called a "Doppler", which, held against the abdomen over the uterus, picks up and transmits sound. Depending on the position of the embryo, the heartbeat can be heard for the first time between 9 and 12 weeks using this device. You can ask to hear this; the sound of your baby's rapid heartbeat can be very moving.

The mother

You will finally begin to feel more in control again. The nausea will begin to subside and you may actually start to feel hungry. Your breasts will be less sensitive, though they will continue to enlarge somewhat throughout pregnancy. Your wide mood swings may become more manageable, your energy will start to return and you will start to feel human again.

At this time, you may first notice that you are starting to develop some of the discomforts of pregnancy – varicose veins, constipation, haemorrhoids (piles). These are discussed in detail in Chapter 3.

You will begin to notice the change in your figure by the beginning of your fourth month. You can expect to gain 2–6 lb (0.90–2.75 kg) in the first trimester, but your change in silhouette will occur even at the low end of the weight-gain range. Your waistline will expand and your lower abdomen will begin to protrude. You probably will not yet have to invest in a new wardrobe, but choose those loose-fitting styles in which you are still comfortable. You may develop stretch marks as your belly, breasts and hips expand (*see* Chapter 3).

Weeks 13–16
The baby

During the fourth month of pregnancy, the foetus will grow to $5\frac{1}{2}$ inches (14 cm) from head to buttocks and will weigh almost $\frac{1}{2}$ lb (0.25 kg). Between 9 and 16 weeks, the head-to-buttock measurement (the crown–rump length) calculated with an ultrasound scan (*see* p. 67) can be used to estimate the foetal age very accurately (give or take four days). The baby's legs, which were still relatively short compared to the body length, will now begin to grow so that they will assume their expected relative length. The head grows at a slower rate so that it becomes more proportional to the body. External genitals can be clearly identified as either male or female. Sometime after 15 weeks, if the baby keeps its legs apart during an

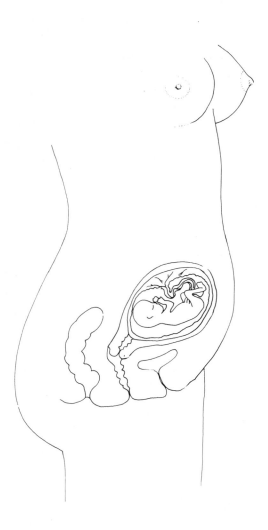

The mother and foetus at 16 weeks.

ultrasound examination, its sex can sometimes be identified. However, this ultrasound identification is not 100 per cent accurate; it is only a visual interpretation that depends on the position of the foetus and the skill of the ultrasound operator.

The mother

If you have already had a baby, you may start to feel the first flutterings of foetal movement ("quickening") by the end of the fourth month. These movements are usually very subtle, often described as "wind" that doesn't pass or like butterflies in your lower abdomen. Because the movements are so subtle, you may not be able to identify them as early in your first pregnancy as you will in subsequent ones. If it is your first pregnancy, don't expect to feel the baby move until at least the 19th or 20th week. At 16 weeks, your uterus can be felt halfway between your pubic bone and belly button.

Weeks 17–24
The baby

The foetus will measure about 10 inches (25 cm) in length and weigh more than $\frac{1}{2}$ lb (0.25 kg). Your doctor or midwife will be able to hear the baby's heartbeat with a foetal stethoscope (foetoscope), though he or she may still choose to use a Doppler (ultrasonic device). The foetus is now covered with a rich, cold cream-like lubricant called the vernix, which protects the baby's skin from the drying effects of the amniotic fluid. By the end of the fourth month, the baby has developed light-coloured eyebrows and eyelashes, and by the end of the fifth month, its body will be covered with a layer of soft downy hair known as lanugo and the scalp will have a covering of hair as well.

The mother

By the end of the fifth month your uterus will be at the level of your belly button and you will feel the flutterings of foetal movement. You will look pregnant and will need a loose-fitting wardrobe. You may want to choose a size that allows you room to grow as your pregnancy progresses. You will probably be feeling terrific, with the nausea and extraordinary fatigue of the first trimester behind you. However, you might feel the uncomfortable stretch of the ligaments which attach your uterus to the abdominal wall and to the groin. This "round ligament pain" is short, sharp and jabbing like a muscle pull. This continues intermittently throughout pregnancy, but is most pronounced in the second trimester.

You will be reassured that the pregnancy is going well by the movements that your baby makes. Remember that each unborn child will have its own rhythm and that it's all right for a foetus to have periods of activity and periods of rest. Your own activity and diet will have a bearing on your baby's activity pattern. Your child's future in-dividuality can first be detected while it is still a foetus. Don't compare this baby's activity or lack of it with your other pregnancies or with any of your friends'. This baby is telling you from the first flutter that it is an individual with its own behaviour pattern. Enjoy it and don't fret over its individual nature.

If you do think you feel a drastic reduction in foetal movement, have something sweet to drink, lie down on your left side and, without any other diversions, concentrate on the baby's movements and count them. You can feel reassured if the baby moves at least four times in an hour. (If it moves 50 times in an hour, that's all right, too; either is acceptable. However, a baby that moves 50 times is not healthier than one that moves less; it is just more active at that time.) If your baby does not move at least four times within that hour, call your doctor.

Weeks 25–28
The baby
By the end of the sixth month the foetus measures somewhere between 11 and 14 inches (28–36 cm) and will weigh about $1\frac{3}{4}$ lb (0.80 kg). It is active and its movements will be much more pronounced. It is now covered in thin, shiny, reddish-brown skin which is covered with vernix. The skin is virtually translucent because there is almost no underlying fat.

Your baby will develop its own individual finger- and toeprints during this month. Its eyelids, which form by the tenth week of foetal life, remain glued shut until approximately the end of the sixth month or beginning of the seventh month. Soon after, it can be seen blinking on an ultrasound scan. If the baby were to be born now, it would have a chance of survival if cared for in an intensive baby-care unit.

The mother
How will you feel now? Probably still very good. Although, by now, the top of your uterus – the *fundus* – will be about three finger-widths

above your belly button, you won't be big enough to feel encumbered, and you will still probably have that second-trimester energy that seems to wane during the third trimester. You might notice the thin white vaginal discharge that is associated with pregnancy (*see* Chapter 3).

The reality of having a baby, of actually bringing a new life into the world and, more precisely, into your family, may hit you by the end of the second trimester (beginning of the seventh month). You may begin to feel emotionally more wary and frightened. Talk to your partner and/or close friends or family about your feelings of apprehension. Start making plans about how you are going to have to adapt your life for this new and totally dependent creature. If you have not done so already, start checking out which childbirth and parenting classes are available and best suited to you. Make a list of your questions and fears for your doctor or midwife so that he or she will be able to address them or direct you to suitable resources.

Weeks 29–35
The baby
Your seventh month will mark the beginning of your third trimester. By the end of this month, your baby will weigh $3\frac{1}{2}$–4 lb (1.6–1.8 kg). During the last trimester, it will be rapidly putting on muscle mass and fat and will gain almost $\frac{1}{2}$ lb (0.25 kg) per week.

The mother
By the seventh month, women will take on distinctive silhouettes – some will carry their babies high, some will carry low, some will appear wide and others will carry "out in front". There is no "normal" way to carry. The sex of your child cannot be predicted by how you carry. Remember that all the "sages" who use this or any other method to predict the sex of your baby have a 50/50 chance of being correct. There is no sure method of predicting the sex of an unborn baby besides genetic screening.

It may seem that your baby is now moving less, and that its movements have changed from large rolling movements to sharper jabbing ones. However, total movement is unlikely to have altered; the reason for this difference is that you will be very aware of the strong movements your baby makes, and they may begin to keep you up at night or awaken you from a sound sleep. Your dreams may become more frequent and more vivid and may also interrupt your restful

31

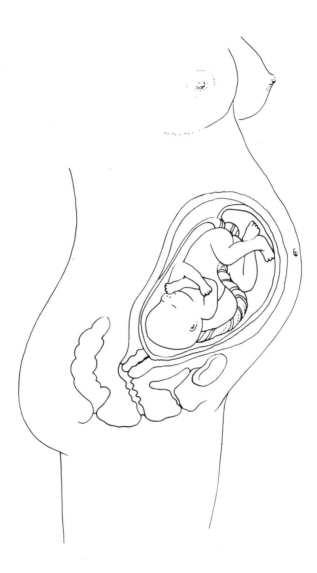

The mother and foetus at 30 weeks.

sleep. This broken sleep is one of the causes for your renewed feeling of fatigue. Also important is the fact that you are now carrying around the extra weight of the baby, placenta, amniotic fluid and enlarged uterus.

You may also start to feel short, rhythmic "blips" of movement in cycles lasting as long as 20 minutes. There is no need to worry – your baby is simply hiccuping! This, along with breathing, thumb sucking and licking motions, can sometimes be seen on ultrasound.

Weeks 36–40
The baby
By the eighth month, the baby will weigh about 5 lb (2.25 kg) or more, and will measure about 18 inches (46 cm) long. During the last two months of pregnancy, the baby puts on fat and muscle mass. The brain, which continues to develop for many months after its birth, matures rapidly during these last weeks. Almost all of the other organ systems are now mature – for example, by the end of the 35th week of pregnancy, 95 per cent of babies will have mature lungs and will not have breathing problems if they are born then. In the last month, the baby will add a final 2 lb (0.90 kg) or more and a final 2 inches (5 cm), reaching the $7\frac{1}{2}$–$7\frac{3}{4}$ lb (3.4–3.5 kg) and 20 inches (50 cm) in length of an average baby born full term.

The mother
With your baby taking up so much room in your belly, you will start to feel more uncomfortable. Your lungs will have a harder time expanding and you may become short of breath. The large uterine size has also pushed the stomach up, causing an increase in heartburn and an inability to eat normal-sized meals. Your protruding abdomen will be putting enormous strain on your lower back. The pressure of the baby on the bladder will again give you the urge to urinate frequently. The pressure of the uterus on the vessels that carry blood returning from the legs and pelvis will increase your chance of developing varicose veins and haemorrhoids, as well as the likelihood of swollen feet and ankles. You will probably be feeling extremely tired. No doubt you will have to start modifying your activities when and if these symptoms occur. Use common sense and listen to your body. And, as always, if you need some help, ask for it.

Added to these physical discomforts are all of your apprehensions about the health of the baby, the oncoming labour and delivery, and

33

the inevitable changes in your life that this baby will bring. As you may well imagine, the last two months can be a trying time. You may also begin to feel impatient for the pregnancy to be over, wondering how 40 weeks could possibly take so long. Your anxiety concerning the pain of labour may mount during the last two months, only to be overtaken by your impatience to have the baby and be finished with being pregnant. This urge to be rid of the pregnancy may become so intense that labour begins to sound like a good time! It seems that this may be nature's way of preparing you for what is ahead: you'll take pain, just get the pregnancy over with.

You may start to feel irregular, intermittent contractions – called *Braxton Hicks contractions* – by the middle of your eighth month. If this is not your first baby, you may start feeling these contractions as early as the beginning of the seventh month. By contracting in this way, the uterus prepares for labour. However, not all women feel these irregular uterine tightenings (*see also* p. 41).

As you enter your last month, you may start to feel less uncomfortable if the baby drops down into the pelvis. This phenomenon, known as *lightening*, does not happen to everyone, but if it does to you, you will find that you have more room for your lungs to expand and for your stomach to fill. As the baby reaches its birth size and the space available to it becomes more confined, you might again notice a change in the quality of the baby's movements. You may even find that these feel unpleasant.

All of the other physical discomforts of pregnancy will probably persist until the birth. During the last six weeks, you may notice an increase in the watery vaginal discharge of pregnancy. Its consistency may thicken, and it may even become blood-tinged. This occurs because the softening of the cervix in preparation for childbirth may colour the discharge with specks or streaks of blood, and this may be particularly noticeable after having sex. This is absolutely normal. If, however, a large gush of bright red blood is expelled from the vagina, call your doctor. If a single "glop" of bloody mucus appears, this is most likely the discharge of the mucous plug from the cervix, which can occur hours to days before labour begins.

During the last weeks of pregnancy, the psychological stresses will usually increase. You will become irritated by such comments as "Are you still pregnant?" or "Haven't you had that baby yet?" If people make such ill-conceived comments to you, don't seethe, remain silent or feel crushed. Tell them that their comments are not

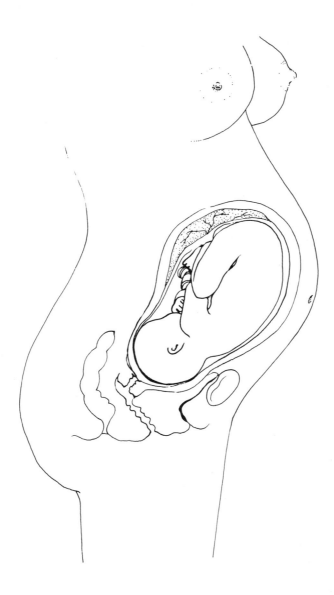

The mother and foetus at 40 weeks. The baby's head has descended into the pelvis — lightening, or engagement — ready to the born.

helpful and what you need is emotional support. They will either back off or offer you the support you need. Comments like these may become even more annoying and anxiety-provoking if you have already gone past your due date. However, this is only an estimated date of delivery, and you could go into labour at any time between two weeks before that date and two weeks after – in other words, 38 to 42 weeks is the length of a normal pregnancy. Indeed, it is quite normal to go as many as 14 days past the due date – and 10 per cent of women do.

Many women work right up until their delivery, finding that this keeps their minds off of their anxieties. However, many others find that they are too physically exhausted or keyed up to continue work. Your body will usually make its needs felt; just listen to it and heed its demands. Most women need some time before the baby is born both to get mentally prepared and to get their homes ready for the new baby. Many expectant mothers spend a lot of time "nesting" before they go into labour, so you may find yourself cleaning and doing house chores like you've never done them before.

At the end of your pregnancy, your cervix will begin to thin out and open, and your baby will drop lower into your pelvis; this is known medically as *cervical effacement, dilatation and foetal descent*. These changes may occur over several days or weeks, but in some women they can happen very rapidly over only a few hours. Every woman and, indeed, every pregnancy is different. Even if your doctor or midwife examines your cervix weekly after your 38th week, he or she will not be able to predict when you will go into labour. There is no schedule, no timetable that will predict the arrival time of your baby. If you are having your child in hospital, keep your suitcase packed and ready to go. Use your last weeks of pregnancy as a time for you and your partner and the rest of your family to enjoy each other's company and prepare for the new baby.

Subsequent pregnancies

If you have had a baby before, some subtle differences will be experienced between this pregnancy and your first. You tend to "show" a few weeks earlier than you did with your first, and the feeling of pressure from the growing baby may be more pronounced – once your abdominal muscles have been stretched, the tone is never 100 per cent the same again.

You may feel a lot more tired because you are caring for other children instead of using the time for yourself. This is especially true if your children are spaced close together and you are looking after a toddler.

With subsequent pregnancies, however, you do tend to be a bit more relaxed about what is happening to you as you are more familiar with what to expect. The discomforts are there but they don't seem as alarming.

CHAPTER THREE

The Discomforts of Pregnancy

Pregnancy is a time of many new physical changes, not all of which are pleasant. Many of the changes are uncomfortable, and some can be painful to some degree. In the following pages, the common discomforts of pregnancy (listed alphabetically) are discussed. You will learn when in pregnancy you can expect them, why they may be happening to you, and some measures you can employ to make yourself more comfortable. There may be times when the symptoms you are experiencing are out of the ordinary. These are also described, and guidance given as to when you should seek medical help.

Backache (high)

A backache that occurs between your shoulder blades is usually caused by the increased size of your breasts. Even women with very small breasts can be troubled with the dramatic increase in size, weight and tenderness of their breasts. Your breasts enlarge at the very beginning of the pregnancy, so you may be troubled by upper backache from the time of your first missed period until your baby is born. If high backache is causing problems the following suggestions may help.

Wear a firm, well-fitting bra. You may need to buy a bigger size, or a different style (such as a long-line bra), than you wore before you were pregnant. Try some on before purchasing any, as some styles will be more comfortable than others. If you plan to breastfeed your baby, you may as well buy nursing bras and wear those during the pregnancy. Your breasts will swell a bit more when your milk comes in after the birth, but after about three days, they will return to the *pregnant* size. Therefore, it would be more economical to wear your nursing bras throughout the pregnancy.

Work on your posture. If you slouch a bit under the weight of your breasts, be conscious of holding your shoulders back and keeping your neck straight. Don't let the weight of your breasts pull you forward.

Stretching exercises (raising your arms over your head) will strengthen the muscles of your upper back, and will help relieve the tension. Warm baths are also wonderfully relaxing and soothing.

When should you be concerned?
• If the pain is severe when you walk or urinate, and is most intense at the base of your ribs (just where your hand reaches), contact your doctor. You may have a urinary tract infection that is travelling up to your kidneys.
• If you get intense upper back pain radiating to the front when you take a breath, especially if it is associated with a general flu-like feeling, again contact your doctor. Pleurisy (inflammation of the membrane surrounding the lungs) may be the cause.
• Constant, severe pain (excruciating and unremitting) under the right ribs towards the end of the pregnancy may be caused by a very serious liver problem. This may also be associated with the symptoms of pre-eclampsia (*see* Chapter 12). This is a rare complication but can be life-threatening if left untreated, so contact your doctor immediately.

Backache (low)

As your baby and uterus grow, your body will experience minor aches and pains as your balance changes to accommodate the weight in front. This is most commonly felt as a low backache. You will use different muscles in your lower back than you do with your non-pregnant figure. This leads to muscle strain, and is most uncomfortable in the third trimester. Another cause of a low backache in pregnancy is the pressure of the baby on the nerve roots in this area which may lead to muscle spasms; these can be very uncomfortable and painful. A third cause of this discomfort is the relaxation effect that the pregnancy hormones have on the ligaments that bind together your pelvic joints. It is for this reason that many women are troubled with a low backache from early on in the pregnancy.

Low backache in pregnancy is a very common and normal occurrence. One of the most important things to consider when trying to alleviate low backpain is good body mechanics. Never bend from the waist to pick up something; always squat and use your leg muscles. When lying on your back, never try to sit up immediately. Always roll on to your side first, then use your elbow to help raise yourself to a sitting position. Assess your posture. Slouching and stooping put more pressure on your lower back, so try to stand tall, and tilt your pelvis forward (the "pelvic tilt" is described in Chapter 5). When you sleep or rest, try lying on your side with a pillow behind your back and one between your legs: this position relieves pressure on your spine, and also allows for optimal blood flow to the baby by removing the bulk of the weight of the pregnant uterus from your major blood vessels. This is also a good time to assess how comfortable your bed is. A firm mattress greatly aids support to your back, but some women find that a waterbed is the answer to their uncomfortable nights.

It is important in pregnancy to maintain some daily exercise to alleviate minor discomforts, and this is especially true for low backache. The toning and strengthening of your muscles will greatly reduce the incidence and intensity of your discomfort.

Avoid shoes with very high heels. They increase the curve of your spine, and put more pressure on your lower back. Maternity girdles are available, and may give the extra support needed to alleviate discomfort. They are especially helpful for women who stand a lot, or who are carrying twins or triplets. If you do have to stand a great deal, try raising one leg and resting it on something about 8 inches (20 cm) high to relieve some of the pressure on your lower back.

As with an upper backache, warm baths work wonders to relieve the tension. Heating pads and hot-water bottles also help and may make you sleep more soundly (be sure to keep the heat low to avoid burns to your skin). If the pain persists despite all of the above measures, try taking two tablets of paracetamol. This is safe to use in pregnancy, and may be all you need to relieve the effects of a stubborn backache.

When should you be concerned?
- If the above relief measures don't work, and you have painful

40

urination, the backache may be caused by a urinary tract infection. Contact your doctor.

● If you have a history of spinal disc problems and the backache becomes intense, contact your doctor.

● If the backache is associated with pressure, and becomes more intense at regular intervals or is just 'different' from what you usually have, it may be a sign of premature labour. Contact your doctor and discuss it.

Braxton Hicks contractions

These contractions are intermittent tightenings of the uterus. They are not associated with pain, and no one really knows exactly why they occur, although it is thought to be the uterus's way of preparing for labour. They can usually be timed, and occur every 5 to 20 minutes. If this is your first baby, you may start to feel the Braxton Hicks contractions about six weeks before your due date. If it is your second or subsequent baby, you may feel them for the last three or four months of your pregnancy. However, some women never experience them.

These contractions are extremely normal and very reassuring for many women as they mean that your body is preparing for labour. If they trouble you, try reducing your activity a bit as this may lessen the intensity of the contractions. Lying on your left side or taking a warm bath may also make them stop.

When should you be concerned?
● If the contractions are increasingly stronger and closer together, and/or become painful, contact your doctor. They may not be Braxton Hicks contractions, but premature labour.

Breast tenderness, changes and discharge

Breast tenderness is usually most troublesome in the first two months of pregnancy, when pregnancy hormones cause the milk ducts to swell, which causes some pain. After the first two months, the breasts remain enlarged, but the discomfort should subside. This is a very normal part of early pregnancy. It is also normal for the veins in your breasts to become more pronounced, appearing to rise to the surface.

The most comforting thing you can do for yourself is to wear a well-fitted supportive bra (*see* Backache [high]).

A yellowish substance may leak from your nipples from about the fifth month on. If it occurs earlier, this is not abnormal, just not as common.

When should you be concerned?
● Any substance leaking from your nipples which is black, green or bloody should be reported to your doctor at once. This may be a sign of breast disease or infection.

Constipation

This is very common in pregnancy, and is caused by several different factors. The pregnancy hormones have a relaxing effect on muscles which makes the digestive tract slow down. This causes constipation, and may be experienced from the very beginning of pregnancy onwards. As your uterus grows, it takes up more and more space which was formerly occupied by the bulk of your intestines. As the intestines become compressed to allow for the growing uterus, the digestive system slows down even more, and intensifies the problem of constipation during the second and third trimesters. Iron supplements are binding and constipating even in the non-pregnant person. If you are taking one or more iron tablets a day, you are even more likely to have trouble with constipation.

Since constipation can lead to other discomforts such as haemorrhoids (*piles*), it is better to take some preventative measures and nip it in the bud. Drink lots and lots of fluids – at least 6–8 large glasses a day. Lack of fluids is the most common cause of constipation in the non-pregnant person, and will compound the problem if you are pregnant. Try drinking warm fruit juice or hot water or tea with lemon first thing in the morning, then wait a half hour before you eat anything else. This will usually stimulate the bowel. Eat as much dietary fibre (roughage) as you can – for instance, salads, raw fruits and vegetables with the peel left on, whole-grain breads and cereals. Take in as many natural sources of iron as possible to avoid the need for iron supplements (*see* Chapter 6).

You may also use a "fibre laxative" (e.g. Metamucil). Dissolve the powder as directed in a glass of juice and follow this with at least two

8-ounce (230 ml) glasses of water. Harsh laxatives and enemas should be avoided. Natural laxatives such as dried fruits, liquorice or prune juice are also helpful. As a special treat, try soaking dried apricots in a little Marsala wine for several days and eat a few of them every day for their natural laxative effect as well as their naturally high iron content.

Faintness

Many women complain of feeling faint when they are pregnant and are concerned that something is wrong. When you are pregnant your blood pressure is a bit lower than it is in your non-pregnant state, and you may experience episodes when it drops even more because of a sudden change in position – for example, when you stand up suddenly, or bend to pick something up. This is common and normal and is relieved when you sit or lie down.

It is also common for the level of sugar in your blood to drop so that you feel faint. This occurs because of the baby's demand for the sugar in your system. This most commonly happens during the late afternoon when most people experience a drop in their blood sugar, and it is intensified in pregnancy. It is a good idea to have a protein snack such as peanuts at about 3.00 p.m. to avoid that late afternoon "crash". Another common time to have a blood sugar drop is about an hour or two after you have eaten something sweet. Your body secretes insulin to deal with the sudden load of sugar it has just received. Because the sugar will then leave the blood very quickly, you may feel weak, sweaty and faint. If this happens, quickly eat some protein with some carbohydrate (for example, peanut butter on cream crackers or some yoghurt); this will break down more gradually and return your blood sugar to normal.

Fatigue

This has got to be the most common complaint in pregnancy. It occurs throughout pregnancy, but is the most severe during the first and third trimesters.

Why pregnant women feel so tired during the first trimester is unclear. The body slows down in general at first, and this may be due to the pregnancy homones. Many women are amazed at how tired they are all the time during the first three months. It may seem that you are longing for your bed all day long, and taking a nap for several hours in the afternoon will hardly seem adequate. The most frustrating thing about this situation is that families seem to run out of patience with this complaint. No one can understand how tired you really are. When they see you vomiting, they believe you – you have "morning sicknes". But the only physical signs of fatigue are the perpetual sight of your body on the sofa, chores left undone, and plans disappointedly forgotten. Your pregnancy barely shows if at all, and so sympathy is often short lived – except from women who have experienced it themselves.

To help cope with this fatigue, try keeping your life simple for a few months. Don't plan any activities that can just as well be put off for a while. Talk to your partner and children about how you feel, and warn them that you will be taking many more rest periods than you usually do. Plan simple, well-balanced meals that are easy to prepare and clean up afterwards. Your doctor will check your blood for anaemia, which can intensify this fatigue.

In the third timester, the tiredness is caused by the extra weight you are carrying around. You'll have 25–30 lb (11–13.5 kg) extra to carry continually, which would be tiring for anyone. The relief measures are the same at this time: rest often, eat well, avoid unnecessary activities and accept help from your friends and family.

Flatulence ("wind")

For the same reasons that you are more prone to constipation when you are pregnant, you are also more prone to having "wind". This occurs throughout the pregnancy but becomes a little worse towards the end. You should avoid foods that cause wind, such as broccoli, cabbage, dried beans, etc. Regular exercise and keeping your bowels regular will help keep the wind moving (*see* Constipation).

Food cravings

Your appetite normally increases when you are pregnant, initially because of the pregnancy hormones, and later because of the demands of the growing foetus on your system. You may find yourself craving unusual foods and being repulsed by food that usually appeals to you. This is all very normal although no one knows exactly why it occurs. Some think that it is because your body is telling you what nutrients it needs. That may be the case if you are craving foods with nutritional value, but is hard to rationalize in cases of a craving for sweets. Eat a well-balanced diet indulging in occasional but reasonable cravings. It really does make you feel better (*see also* Taste changes).

When should you be concerned?
● If you are craving non-food substances such as clay or newsprint, let your doctor know about it. It is thought that anaemia may be the cause of what is known as *pica*, the craving of non-food substances.

Gums (sore or bleeding)

All of your mucous membranes lining the inside of your body and your nose and mouth become more sensitive when you are pregnant. Due in part to the extra fluid in your cells during pregnancy, this is a normal condition, but can be irritating. Your gums may become sore at various times during the pregnancy, but most commonly in the second trimester. To prevent very inflamed gums, have a dental check-up early in the pregnancy to have your teeth properly cleaned and any fillings taken care of. Use a soft-bristled toothbrush to prevent bleeding, and rinse your mouth with warm salt water ($\frac{1}{2}$ teaspoon salt to 8 fl oz water) several times a day.

When should you be concerned?
● If you have intense pain in your mouth, have your dentist take a look; you may be harbouring an infection.

Haemorrhoids (piles)

These are varicose veins in the rectum (back passage), and can become extremely swollen and painful. They can be caused by the pressure of the baby in your pelvis towards the end of pregnancy, but you may have trouble with them throughout pregnancy if you are constipated.

If you are troubled with haemorrhoids, it is imperative to get your bowels regulated (*see* Constipation). The weight of the baby coupled with the pressure of hard stool in the rectum is bad news for the woman with haemorrhoids. Soaking in a warm bath will enhance circulation and soften the haemorrhoidal tissue; this is usually very comforting and soothes the pain. You can make a compress with witch hazel (available from chemists and healthfood shops) and place it against the haemorrhoids for 10–15 minutes at a time. This will shrink them, and make it easier to push any external ones back inside with your finger. (If you prefer a cold compress, keep the witch hazel in the refrigerator.) Epsom salts may also be used to make a compress if you prefer. Commercial preparations are available and may be prescribed by your doctor. They are all aimed at shrinking the haemorrhoids enough so that they may be pushed back inside.

When should you be concerned?
● Occasionally, a haemorrhoid becomes clotted (thrombosed). This means that a blood clot has formed in the vein, and it becomes hard, swollen and excruciatingly painful. You may also have considerable bleeding with a haemorrhoid like this. Contact your doctor. Thrombosed haemorrhoids may need to be lanced to remove the clots. This may sound horrible, but the procedure is actually very quick and simple, and it brings instant relief.

Headaches

Even women who are not prone to headaches usually experience them when they are pregnant. There is possibly a hormonal factor involved, but there are also a few other causes. Your sinuses will be much more sensitive and swell and drain more readily when you are pregnant, and this most definitely can lead to a headache. The headaches are usually more frequent in the early part of pregnancy but may occur at any time.

If it is possible, lie down for a while in a warm, quiet, dark room. This may be all it takes to relieve the pain. Sometimes a snack helps, and peppermint tea is said to relieve headache pain. If the pain is severe, paracetamol is safe to take even in early pregnancy. If it is a sinus headache, breathing in steam helps. You could also try compressing the sinuses with a hot compress (covering an area extending from above the eyebrows to 1 inch/2.5 cm below the cheek-bones), or taking a mild decongestant such as Sudafed or Dimotapp.

When should you be concerned?
- If you are 20 or more weeks pregnant and you have a throbbing headache associated with blurry vision, call your doctor. This may be associated with high blood pressure or neurological problems.

Heartburn

This is common in pregnancy and can make life miserable if you have a bad case of it. There are a few things that cause it, one being the relaxation of the muscle that prevents the food coming back up from the stomach into the oesophagus (gullet). This relaxation is an effect of the pregnancy hormones, and they also slow digestion, delaying the emptying of the stomach. These factors, combined with the increasing lack of space for the stomach due to the growing uterus, can make for unpleasant meal times and bedtimes.

There are many measures you can take to cope with this discomfort. Eat smaller more frequent meals to avoid overloading the stomach. Avoid fatty and greasy foods, since fat decreases the ability of the stomach to move food through. Avoid very cold foods as these inhibit the digestive juices. Limit the amount of fluids you drink with your meals: they fill your stomach quickly, and may inhibit the secretion of gastric juices. Identify which foods make your heartburn worse and avoid them. Very spicy foods should also be avoided. Good posture will give your stomach the optimal room to function. Don't lie down flat for a few hours after you eat, but prop yourself up with a few pillows; this will prevent the food from travelling back into the oesophagus. Antacids may be used if they help, and some even have extra calcium in them. Ask your doctor which ones he or she recommends.

When should you be concerned?
- If heartburn pain is persistent and severe, and radiates to your neck, contact your doctor. It is possible that a hiatus hernia (when part of the stomach slips into the chest through the hole in the diaphragm meant for the oesophagus) may cause such severe symptoms.

Insomnia

This is a very common complaint in pregnancy, and could account for some of the fatigue that is felt during the day. It occurs more often towards the end of pregnancy when you are physically uncomfortable and rolling over is a major effort. The movements of the baby may also prevent you from falling asleep or wake you. Pregnant women are also more prone to nightmares (*see* Nightmares).

If you have trouble falling asleep or become very wakeful during the night, try taking a warm bath before retiring. This is very relaxing, and may be all you need to have a good night's sleep. A warm drink before bed can also enhance sleep, especially milk or camomile tea. Use as many pillows as it takes to make yourself comfortable in bed, including one for between your knees and one behind your back. Rest during the day may also help you sleep better; contrary to what you may believe, extreme fatigue may actually prevent sleep. Don't do any exercises within two hours of going to bed; this will stimulate you and keep you awake. Lastly, don't eat anything sweet during the evening hours. The extra sugar in your system will make the baby active, just what you don't want then.

Itching (skin, vagina, vulva)

Many women complain of itchy skin, or itchiness around the genital area. The cause of this is not exactly known, although you do sweat more when you are pregnant, and itching across the abdomen may be caused by the stretching of the skin. If itching is not associated with a rash or skin condition, don't worry about it. Maintain good hygiene, but creams and lotions won't help.

The itchiness around the vagina may be caused by the increase in vaginal secretions (*see* Vaginal discharge). Again, there isn't much you can do about it. Douching won't help and is not recommended.

Leg cramps

The pressure of the enlarging uterus on the pelvic blood vessels and on the nerve endings that go through the pelvis and down the leg can lead to more frequent leg cramps. It is also thought that a lack of calcium can cause this. Besides eating a well-balanced diet, a good general exercise routine may help to prevent leg cramps.

Towards the end of pregnancy, cramps may increase in frequency, and happen usually when you are lying in bed and stretching your legs with your toes pointed. To avoid this, always sit up to do your stretching exercises, and flex your feet and toes back towards your legs if cramping occurs.

"Morning sickness", *see* Nausea and vomiting

Nasal stuffiness and bleeding

As mentioned under "Gums", all of your mucous membranes become sensitive and more readily inflamed when you are pregnant, partly because of the increased blood flow to those membranes. Your sinuses seem to drain and produce mucus even if you don't have a head cold. As a result, "post-nasal drip" is very common and may be extremely annoying, especially if you are having trouble with nausea. Nasal stuffiness occurs throughout pregnancy. In the winter months, when the air is dry from central heating, there may be some bleeding when you blow your nose. If this happens, don't be alarmed if it is only a small amount. Try using a vaporizer or humidifier, or just boil some water on the cooker and breathe in the steam.

During pregnancy, it is also common to have nosebleeds that are mild and infrequent and which occur because the inside of the nose is irritated. To stop a nosebleed, lean backwards and pinch the soft part of the nose just below the bridge for at least ten minutes.

When should you be concerned?
● If you are having severe nosebleeds that take longer than ten minutes to stop, consult your doctor. This may be an indication that there is a problem with your blood.

Nausea and vomiting

The cause of the nausea and vomiting that can occur in early pregnancy (commonly known as "morning sickness") is not certain, although there are several current theories. Some researchers believe that the cause is high levels of the hormone oestrogen in the body at that time, and others feel that it is a lack of sugar in the blood caused by the demands of the foetus's developing nervous system.

This is a problem of early pregnancy, generally only the first trimester. It usually starts about two weeks after the first missed period, and disappears at 12–13 weeks. A few women are troubled with it until 18–20 weeks, but that is much less common.

Nausea can be very debilitating especially if you are also vomiting. It's depressing to go to bed and dread the morning because you know you'll feel so sick. Most of the time, the nausea is at its worst in the morning. If you can get something into your system (anything that appeals to you) rather quickly after rising, you will usually feel better. It is often suggested that you keep crackers on your bedside table, so you can eat something before you get out of bed. Sometimes this works and sometimes it doesn't, but it's worth a try.

If you suffer from nausea in early pregnancy, give in to your cravings. They usually make you feel much better, even if they're not nutritionally recommended. Coke syrup, which is found in Coca-Cola, is known to settle upset stomachs, so drinking cola helps sometimes. If that doesn't appeal to you, try any sweet liquid such as fruit juice or ginger ale. Don't let yourself get too hungry; an empty stomach seems to make the nausea much worse. Eat small frequent meals, and snack often during the day.

Try to maintain your daily regime during the first trimester, with a few extra rest periods thrown in. Getting out of the house usually helps divert your attention; sitting at home and focusing on how you feel will make the situation seem endless. This is a very normal, albeit uncomfortable part of pregnancy, and, in fact, it is one of the signs of a healthy pregnancy. (This does not mean you should worry that your pregnancy is not healthy if you are one of the lucky few who escape this fate!)

If the vitamins you have been prescribed by the antenatal clinic are compounding your nausea, talk to your doctor about waiting until the nausea subsides before resuming them. After all, it is counter-productive to take in something only to throw it up later on.

When should you be concerned?
If you are holding nothing down, and are beginning to get de-hydrated, contact your doctor or midwife. In extreme cases, some

women need to be hospitalized and given intravenous fluids to deal with the condition.

Nightmares

Many women have very vivid dreams while pregnant, and nightmares are very common. This is true throughout the nine months, and may be due in part to the hormonal changes within you. It may also be because you are having to grapple with a great many impending changes, which can cause some anxiety. Many of these anxieties are manifested in dreams.

Dreaming that the baby is born deformed is very common, and is not a premonition of things to come. Rather, this is a subconscious expression of your anxiety. As your baby grows and you feel more and more uncomfortable, it is not uncommon to have dreams about being locked in a cupboard, or lost in a city, or being in a situation that you cannot get out of. This is an expression of your feelings of being stifled by your cumbersome size. It may also symbolize the anxiety you have about your impending loss of freedom.

There is nothing you can do about your nightmares or dreams, but understanding them and knowing that they are normal may help.

Numbness and tingling of fingers and toes

In the third trimester, you may experience some tingling in your fingers and toes. It is more common in your fingers if your posture is poor, or if your breasts are very large. Both of these put a strain on the nerves that affect your hands, and they become tingly. This is also common while breastfeeding, because of the increased weight of your breasts and the curve of your body while nursing. If the tingling is restricted to your hands and fingers, watching your posture and wearing a supportive bra may help.

If you are experiencing tingling in your toes and feet, it is most likely caused from the weight of the baby on the nerves in your groin which affect your feet. Lying on your side periodically throughout the day, and getting the weight of the baby off those nerves may bring some relief. It is normal to have to endure some numbness and tingling in the latter part of pregnancy.

When should you be concerned?
● Excessive swelling may be the cause of the discomfort you are experiencing (*see* Swelling). Consult your doctor or midwife if excessive swelling occurs as you may need to be monitored for pre-eclampsia.
● If the tingling in your hands becomes so uncomfortable that it wakes you up, or if you wake with numb hands, consult your doctor. This may indicate the more serious problem of carpal tunnel syndrome, when one of the nerves to the hand comes under pressure in the wrist.

Perineal pressure

During the second and third trimester, you may feel some pressure in your perineum – the fleshy area around the vagina and anus – from the weight of your growing baby and the swelling of the mucous membranes lining your vagina and vulva. This is normal as long as it is not painful. If it bothers you, spend more time lying on your side to relieve the pressure of the baby and improve the circulation. Painful pressure is often constipation. However, as you reach the end of pregnancy, it may be a sign of rapidly progressing labour.

When should you be concerned?
● If you are not constipated and feel a very definite, painful pressure, call your doctor or midwife right away.

Perspiration

The increased level of the hormone progesterone in your system can cause occasional hot flushes, like those that may occur during menopause. Progesterone also increases the amount you perspire considerably. This happens throughout the pregnancy and afterwards. It is very normal and nothing can be done to prevent it. Be aware that there is a sound reason for it, adjust your wardrobe accordingly, and maintain good hygiene.

Piles, *see* Haemorrhoids

Pubic pain

During the last eight weeks of pregnancy, the pressure of the baby on your pubic area (in the front of the pelvis, where the hipbones meet beneath the abdomen) can become very uncomfortable, especially when standing or walking for long periods. For some, it becomes downright painful. One effect of the hormone progesterone is to soften the cartilage between the two sides of the pelvis, allowing it to move far more freely. This can lead to muscle strain, and thus to pain. If you are bothered with this, a maternity girdle may prove to be very supportive and comforting. Avoid standing for excessive periods; this may not be the time to visit a zoo or museum. If your job requires standing for long periods, some modification of your schedule or where you work may need to be made.

When should you be concerned?
• If the pain becomes intense and is not relieved by the above measures, contact your doctor. You may have a urinary tract infection, or a separation (not just a softening) of your pelvic bone (*symphysis pubis*).

Round ligament pain

The uterus is suspended from the abdominal walls by the round ligaments. As the uterus grows during pregnancy, these ligaments stretch and occasionally go into spasm, which results in what is known as "round ligament pain" – like a "stitch" in your side. These pains may occur in the first trimester, but they are most likely from the middle of the second trimester to the end of the pregnancy. The pain is usually sharp and pulling or stabbing, and doubles you over for a minute. It is most likely to be brought on when you move suddenly, as you do when you sneeze or cough or stand up quickly. It also often happens when you roll over in bed, when it can wake you out of a sound sleep.

If you are troubled with a lot of round ligament pain, warm baths will relax you and ease it a bit. Let your body react naturally to the pain: your body will instinctively curl around the area that hurts, which will ease the spasm. These pains are a very normal part of pregnancy.

When should you be concerned?

● If the pain is continuous and lasts longer than three minutes, and is not relieved with a hot soak or when you lie on your side with your knees bent, contact your doctor. Round ligament pain may not be the cause of that pain.

Salivation (excessive)

Women normally salivate much more when they are pregnant, and some find this exceedingly unpleasant. It can also lead to an increase in the amount of nausea experienced in the first trimester, and may make food seem somewhat less appealing. It is at its most severe in the first trimester, and usually isn't a problem after the second trimester. Some people think that additional starch in the diet (e.g. potatoes, bread) is the cause of increased salivation, but this has not been substantiated.

If it really bothers you, you could try limiting the amount of starch you take in and see if this works. You can also rinse your mouth out with mouthwash or salt water ($\frac{1}{2}$ teaspoon salt to 8 fl oz warm water) several times a day, as this will alleviate the unpleasant taste associated with the excess saliva.

Shortness of breath

During the latter part of the second trimester and during the third trimester, your uterus grows so that it limits the space your lungs have to expand. The uterus also exerts pressure on your diaphragm (the large muscle between the chest and the abdomen) which makes normal breathing a little more difficult. Such shortness of breath is very common and not an indication of a respiratory ailment. It is normal, especially if you are exerting yourself physically. Climbing stairs may seem like a big chore now, and this may be a very frustrating feeling. Listen to your body and limit your activity to what you feel comfortable doing. Do slow, deep-breathing exercises to enhance your lung capacity. At night, you may need a few extra pillows under your head and shoulders to relieve the pressure of the baby on your diaphragm. The shortness of breath may be relieved somewhat at the end of the third trimester if the baby drops down into your pelvis.

Skin changes (pigmentation and stretch marks)

The skin changes of pregnancy are another result of the high levels of the hormones oestrogen and progesterone present in your system. Your nipples may darken in colour and become larger. Moles or other darkly pigmented areas may also become larger and darker. Exposure to the sun will have a completely different effect on your skin now that you are pregnant. Patches of dark skin may appear on your face; this is commonly known as the "mask of pregnancy" and medically as *chloasma*. The narrow line on your abdomen that travels from your navel to your pubic hair may also darken, and may become thicker with hair; this is known as the *linea nigra*. These changes are all very normal, and will fade (though not disappear) after your baby is born. The only preventive measures you can take are to limit your time in the sun, and to use a good sun-screening cream. This will prevent a drastic effect, but won't completely eliminate the hormonal effect.

Stretch marks are another skin change occurring from late in the second trimester and throughout the remainder of the pregnancy. They are not preventable nor are they predictable. These pink or pale-coloured lines on the belly, breasts and/or hips are caused by rapid growth and the stretch of the skin, as well as by certain hormonal effects of pregnancy. About 85 per cent of women (that is, those with a genetic predisposition) will develop stretch marks. There are no creams, lotions, exercises or massages that will prevent or get rid of them. Don't be hoodwinked by the advertising ploy of some useless and expensive skin product aimed at the pregnant population. Just know that at the end of your pregnancy, your skin will regain its elasticity and the stretch marks will fade over time into thin, barely noticeable, somewhat shiny skin-coloured streaks. A supportive partner, a healthy diet, and a positive self-image will help you in accepting the change.

Swelling

As described in Chapter 2, your blood volume increases by half again its normal volume. This, combined with the increased pressure from the growing foetus on the major blood vessels in your groin, will account for a certain amount of swelling, especially in your feet and ankles. The hormones present in your system also make you retain a small amount of fluid all over your body, resulting in tight finger rings and a face that is fuller than usual. These changes generally occur from about the middle of the second trimester through to the end of pregnancy. If your baby is due during the summer months, or if you live in a hot climate, the swelling may be even more marked.

A certain amount of swelling is expected and normal during pregnancy. The following suggestions will help you to keep the discomfort at a minimum. During the day, keep your legs raised as much as possible. Lying down on your left side is best because it keeps the weight of the baby off your major blood vessels. (The major vessels travel down your torso just to the right of centre; thus, left-sided rest is best.) If lying down during the day is not practical because you are working, sitting with your legs raised is good, too. Putting them on a stool under your desk may be possible if you have a desk job, or you could put them up on another chair in the employees' lounge. Ensure that your clothes are not tight and restrictive, especially in the groin, as that would inhibit circulation even more. Wear loose clothing; it is much more comfortable. Perhaps surprisingly, it is important to increase your fluid intake: with any swelling, it is important to keep your kidneys flushed.

When should you be concerned?
● If obvious swelling occurs all at once and is prominent in your face and fingers, contact your doctor. This may be a symptom of pre-eclampsia and require medical attention immediately.
● If the swelling increases dramatically and you are urinating less and less, contact your doctor. This may be an indication that there is kidney disease, possibly from toxaemia (*see* Chapter 12).

Taste changes

You may notice that, when you are pregnant, food tastes different than it used to. This is extremely common, but the exact reason for it is unknown. It may be due to the hormones of pregnancy, or the extra saliva secreted in pregnancy may affect the taste of certain foods (*see* Salivation [excessive]). Whatever the cause, be assured that it is normal, and there isn't anything you can do about it. It disappears after the baby is born (*see also* Food cravings.)

Urinary frequency

At the very beginning of pregnancy, the growing uterus is close to the bladder and may rest right on top of it. At about 14 weeks, the uterus rises up out of the pelvis and off the bladder, and the pressure is relieved. Then, in late pregnancy, the baby's head presses against the bladder. During these periods – early and late pregnancy – you may feel the need to urinate very frequently, yet there is only a small amount of urine each time. This is a very normal condition at these times, and not much can be done about it except to limit your fluid intake when you know that you won't be near a lavatory.

When should you be concerned?
• If the urinary frequency is associated with burning on urination, or with lower abdominal cramping, fever or blood in the urine, contact your doctor or midwife. These are signs of a urinary tract infection, and you may need treatment with an antibiotic.

Vaginal discharge

The increased blood supply to your vaginal area may account for the increase in vaginal secretions – called *leukorrhoea* – during pregnancy. This thin, white vaginal discharge is normal and occurs throughout the pregnancy, increasing in the third trimester. Some women are bothered by this change, and feel uncomfortable. Wearing cotton underwear or no underwear will allow air to dry it out; alternatively, you can wear a panty liner. Loose clothing will allow the maximum air flow, and decrease the amount of perspiration secreted. You should not douche as this alters the normal flora of the vagina, and can actually cause infections.

When should you be concerned?
• If the vaginal discharge is a colour other than white or yellow, or has a foul odour, let your doctor or midwife know. You may have an infection.
• If the discharge is white and thick, and your vulva is itchy and sore, you may have a yeast infection. Contact your doctor or midwife.
• If the discharge is very watery (like urine) and profuse (trickling

down your leg), it is possible that your "waters" have broken – that is, the fluid-filled amniotic sac surrounding the baby may have ruptured. Contact your doctor or midwife as your baby is now less protected from infection; in addition, you may go into labour soon. There is also a risk of the cord slipping below the baby, causing potential problems.

Varicose veins

Pregnant women are susceptible to varicose veins in two different places – in the legs and in the vulva. There are a few causes. First of all, the hormone progesterone relaxes the walls of the blood vessels in the pelvic region and the legs, and this allows them to stretch more readily. As a result, the flaps (valves) that stop the backflow of blood no longer meet, thus allowing blood to collect in little swollen lakes. Later in the pregnancy, the pressure of the growing uterus impedes the return of blood to the major vessels, and impedes the flow of the blood returning in the veins. And there is also a family tendency for varicose veins; if your mother had them, you are more likely to have them.

There are several measures you can take to relieve the discomfort of varicose veins. Wear support tights. These come specially made for pregnant women, and also offer support to your abdomen. Preferably put them on before you get out of bed in the morning. Take frequent rest periods during the day with your feet raised above the level of your waist. Don't wear clothes that bind, or cut off your circulation. If you have varicose veins in your vulva, wear a maxi-pad with the support tights to give this area extra support. Try to avoid being constipated, as this just adds more pressure (*see* Constipation).

When should you be concerned?
● If you suddenly get severe calf or leg pain that increases when you point your toes back toward your knees, contact your doctor or midwife at once. This is a sign of a deep vein thrombosis (blood clot).
● If you get a reddened area on the skin that is painful and warm to the touch, contact your doctor immediately. This also may be a thrombosis. Do not rub the area since you do not want to dislodge the clot.
● If your skin starts to break down and develops ulcers, this means

your circulation is impaired. If this happens, you need medical attention immediately.

Vomiting, *see* Nausea and vomiting

Walking difficulties

The combination of relaxed pelvic joints (*see* Backache [low]) with the extra weight of the baby in your abdomen may cause an alteration in your gait – that is, the way you walk. This can occur late in the third trimester, and may become marked when the head of the baby drops down into the pelvis. It is more common in short women, and disappears after the baby is born. It helps to have good posture, and wear comfortable, low-heeled, well-fitting shoes.

CHAPTER FOUR

Antenatal Testing

There are many tests that can offer you and your doctor or midwife information about the health of both you and your baby. A few of these are carried out on a routine basis (e.g. a blood test for syphilis), but others may only be recommended for women who may be at risk of certain conditions. Your doctor or midwife will generally recommend a particular test because he or she believes that the results will have a bearing on your pregnancy. If you have any questions about why a test is being recommended or if you wonder whether you should have a specific test, feel free to ask. Remember that your doctor or midwife and you share the same basic goal – a healthy baby and a healthy mother.

At your routine antenatal visits, the doctor and midwife will assess how your pregnancy is progressing.

● *Is the baby growing?* This is determined by assessing the size of your uterus, by feeling and measuring your belly, at each visit.

● *How are you doing?* Your weight, blood pressure and urine are checked at each visit to screen out any developing medical problems and to assess your nutritional status.

● *Does your baby seem to be doing OK?* The baby's heartbeat will be listened to and your belly will be felt to check the baby's outline and position. This assessment is done with simple, basic tools, including hands. You may require very little additional testing beyond these various assessments. However, if what is found during the examination deviates from the expected norm, then further and more sophisticated tests may be necessary.

There are three basic kinds of tests: basic information tests; specific tests which may be required if you or your baby develop a problem; and screening tests. Screening tests are very common in all branches of medicine but particularly so in obstetrics (medical care in pregnancy and childbirth). They are designed to look at all pregnant women in an effort to discover which of them may be affected by a particular problem (e.g. Down's syndrome). This does *not* mean that, if the results of your initial screening test are abnormal, your baby is abnormal, or that you are sick. What it does mean is that you are a candidate for further testing.

You may ask, "Why not have everyone go on to the second stage instead of frightening those people who fail the first stage?" First of all, nobody "fails" a screening test; this is not like a spelling test. If the results of a screening test (the first stage) are abnormal, this only means that you are a candidate for a more sophisticated test. Why not start with the more sophisticated test? Because it usually requires more resources to perform – that is, it may cost more, be more time consuming, take a more skilled person to perform – or it may have more associated risks. The screening test, if negative, tells you that you are probably not affected by the problem for which you are being tested and will therefore require no further tests. For example, to screen people for diabetes, first a simple one-hour screen is used, a test in which a small but specific amount of sugar (glucose) is given to each person, followed after one hour by a blood test to determine the level of sugar in the blood (blood glucose). Research has shown what level is normal, and if your test result is higher than that level, then you are a candidate for the more extensive three-hour screening test. Therefore, if after the first screening test your level is determined to be higher than the acceptable norm, *you have not failed the test*; nor does it mean that you are a diabetic. It only means that it would be worthwhile including you in the more sophisticated testing in an effort to find those members of the original group who are indeed diabetic.

The first antenatal tests

Weight, blood pressure and urine checks
At your routine antenatal visits, the doctor or midwife will check your weight, blood pressure and your urine.

Your weight is checked so that, over several visits, the overall trend of your weight gain can be evaluated and dietary recommendations can be made if necessary. If sustained weight loss occurs, the doctor or midwife will evaluate your diet and how much exercise you do and will make recommendations. Remember that pregnancy is not a time to diet or lose weight, and sustained weight loss should be investigated. In addition, sudden large jumps in weight gain may indicate that a problem is developing (such as toxaemia), and the doctor or midwife will want to investigate this further.

Your blood pressure will be checked at every visit as well as during labour. Your normal blood pressure range will be established, and any wide deviation from that range will be evaluated. In particular, a sudden rise may indicate developing toxaemia, which would require prompt treatment.

Your urine will be routinely tested for the presence of sugar, which, if found in substantial amounts, may indicate diabetes. If protein is found in significant quantities, there may be reason to suspect a possible urinary tract infection or the development of toxaemia.

Blood tests

At your first antenatal appointment, the doctor or midwife will order a group of blood tests. These will include a *complete blood count* (CBC) which will measure the level of red blood cells (too low indicates anaemia), the level of white blood cells (too high may mean an infection is brewing or is present), the specific kind of white blood cells present (which, if an infection is present, may indicate whether it is caused by bacteria, viruses or parasites) and the number of platelets (cells involved in blood clotting). It is very important to keep track of the level of red blood cells throughout your pregnancy because pregnant women have a tendency to become anaemic. It is for this reason that the CBC may be repeated later in pregnancy.

Your *blood type* will also be determined on the first visit. The two main components tested for are those of the ABO group (blood type A, type B, type AB and type O) and those of the Rh group (Rh positive or Rh negative). The blood can contain many other factors but they are rare and it is unlikely that they will cause any problems during pregnancy or childbirth.

The initial blood screen includes two tests for contagious diseases: a screening test for syphilis, and a test to ascertain whether you are immune to *rubella* (German measles).

Syphilis is a disease which can adversely affect the baby if left untreated, and treatment of the mother prevents the birth of an infected newborn. If your syphilis test comes back positive, do not immediately assume that you have this sexually transmitted disease. The results of the test may be distorted if you have certain other medical conditions (e.g. Reynaud's disease, lupus, etc.) If you do, there may be a factor in your blood which interferes with the test's ability to interpret properly whether or not you have syphilis, thereby possibly giving a false positive result. In those very rare cases, your blood would be sent for the more specific test for syphilis (*see also* Chapter 12).

Your rubella status is also determined during the first antenatal visit. If it is discovered that you are not immune, you should avoid exposure to people with the virus because, although rubella is a very mild illness, if it is contracted by a baby in the womb in the first three months of pregnancy, it can be very severely damaged. Fortunately, this virus is becoming more rare because of widespread immunization and it is less likely that you will be exposed to it. Despite this, women who are not immune should be immunized after giving birth. However, even if you have tested as immune once, it is important to be tested again when contemplating a future pregnancy as, in rare cases, immunity can disappear (*see also* Chapter 12).

Screening for the liver disease *hepatitis type B* is now also routinely undertaken for all pregnant women, and further blood tests may be ordered closer to the birth, especially for women who may be at risk of contracting the disease during pregnancy. Hepatitis type B is transmitted via contact with infected blood, saliva, urine, vaginal secretions and semen. It is also commonly seen in those who take drugs and share dirty needles, and among men who indulge in homosexual behaviour; it is also common in certain parts of the world. It is very important to know prior to childbirth if a woman has the active disease or is (perhaps unknowingly) carrying the active hepatitis B viral particle. If a woman is a carrier, it is likely that she will pass the particle to the baby at the time of delivery. In that case, the baby can be given a special type of vaccination (immune globulin) immediately after birth and hepatitis vaccine within one week and again at one month of life, and thus be protected from getting hepatitis type B.

You may be thinking that this has no bearing on you because you know that you don't have and have never had hepatitis, and in all likelihood, you are right. However, hepatitis, like many other viruses, can strike in such a mild form that you may never be aware that you have been exposed to or contracted the virus. Even in that case, you would not necessarily become a carrier. This only happens when, after being infected by hepatitis type B (no matter how mildly), the person who contracts it does not fully form all of the antibodies to kill off the virus; then that person is in danger of carrying the infective viral particle for the rest of his or her life. Although you may think that this scenario is rare, in many parts of the world – for example China, South-east Asia, India, Pakistan, the sub-Sahara – it is very common. Testing of all pregnant women is now recommended because even if the chances of carrying the hepatitis B virus are not great, the risk to the babies of infected mothers *is* very high. In addition, there now exists an easily administered and very effective treatment.

Other blood tests that may be done are those to detect toxoplasmosis and cytomegalovirus infection (*see* Chapter 12).

AIDS (HIV) testing

Routine mandatory screening for the virus which causes AIDS – the HIV, human immunodeficiency virus – has been much discussed in recent years, but mandatory screening has not yet become a reality. If it does, it will pose an enormous number of ethical questions. Because there is widespread fear of and discrimination against people who have AIDS as well as against those who carry the virus but have not developed any symptoms of the disease, all testing should be anonymous and all test centres should provide pre- and post-test counselling. Confidentiality of test results is difficult to ensure, and thus far, no reasonable system for testing has been developed.

There is also the possibility that, some time in the future, blood tests for HIV may be carried out on the samples given by all pregnant women at antenatal clinics. All the ways of identifying who gave which samples would be eliminated, as the results from these tests would be used simply to detect the incidence of the virus within the population. However, ethical questions remain: is it right to discover that a woman is unknowingly carrying the virus and not tell her?

Voluntary testing is widely available and should provide pre- and post-test counselling and confidentiality as well. The initial screening test currently available has about a 15 per cent false positive rate. All positive tests are followed up by a more accurate test, and if both tests are positive, then the person being tested almost certainly carries the HIV virus. The latency period for women (that is, the time it takes from contracting the virus to developing symptoms of the disease) can be as long as ten years or perhaps even longer. This, as well as the 50 per cent chance of passing the virus to the unborn baby, poses a large dilemma to infected women who are contemplating pregnancy or those who discover that they are already pregnant.

Cervical smear test

A cervical smear test is also performed when you are first examined at the antenatal clinic. It is important to remember that all facets of your health should be maintained while you are pregnant; in fact, the hallmark of good antenatal care is to maintain the best possible physical and mental health in the mother so that she, in turn, may provide the best possible environment for the growth and well-being of her baby. That is why routine women's health care, such as cervical screening, is performed.

Clearly if you are harbouring any abnormal cells or infection in your cervix, this should be discovered at your first visit so that it can be properly monitored and/or treated. An abnormal (positive) cervical smear may mean that a repeat smear needs to be performed later in the pregnancy, or, in some cases, that colposcopy needs to be performed. Colposcopy is a test whereby the cervix is examined under high magnification so that the abnormal cells may be located exactly, mapped for future evaluation, and examined for their severity. If pre-cancerous or cancerous cells are discovered, you will obviously want to discuss with your doctor or midwife how you should proceed with the pregnancy and how your delivery might be affected.

Later tests

Alpha-foetoprotein (AFP)

At about 16 weeks, a test for AFP (alpha-foetoprotein) will be carried out. This blood test was originally designed to screen for defects in the baby's nervous system which allow spinal fluid to leak out into the amniotic fluid – that is, open neural tube defects such as spina bifida, open hydrocephaly and meningomyelocoel. Since it was introduced, however, it has been found that the AFP test can indicate other problems that may complicate pregnancy.

First of all, what is AFP? It is a protein made by the foetus which can be detected in the mother's blood, where it is called "maternal serum alpha-foetoprotein (MSAFP). It is the MSAFP which can be measured between 16 and 19 weeks. During this period, the amount of this protein produced by the baby rises so rapidly that what is normal (within upper and lower limits) can be established week by week.

If the measurement of your MSAFP is above or below the limits of what is considered normal for the length of your pregnancy (as well as for your height, weight, race and whether or not you are diabetic), this does *not* mean that your baby is abnormal. It only means that you are a candidate for further testing. In fact, 90 per cent of babies whose mothers have an abnormal MSAFP are quite normal.

A low MSAFP may indicate that the risk of your baby being born with Down's syndrome (previously known as "mongolism") is as great as that of a woman aged 35; it does not mean that your baby has Down's syndrome. However, you may then be offered amniocentesis (*see below*) in an effort to determine your baby's exact genetic make-up and to rule out Down's syndrome. In addition, the reverse may be true: because MSAFP is far from perfect at identifying those at risk of Down's syndrome, a normal MSAFP does not guarantee that the baby does not carry the genes for Down's syndrome.

An elevated MSAFP indicates that further testing would be in order to rule out a neural tube defect. This may include amniocentesis and/or ultrasound (*see below*). An ultrasound may reveal twins; obviously two babies make more protein than one and therefore an elevated MSAFP may be the first clue that you're carrying twins. Also, an elevated MSAFP may indicate that you are further along in your pregnancy than you suspected. Therefore, if your MSAFP is elevated for a 16-week pregnancy, ultrasound may show that you are really 18 or 20 weeks pregnant and, thus, your MSAFP is entirely normal for the true length of your pregnancy.

The AFP can also be measured in the amniotic fluid obtained by amniocentesis. If a normal amount is found, it is almost sure the baby does *not* have a neural tube defect. If the amniotic fluid AFP is elevated, it still does not mean that the baby has a neural tube defect. There are other factors which can elevate this protein; however, if it is high, then a careful look at the baby's brain and spine is warranted.

What has recently been discovered is that those pregnancies in which there has been a high MSAFP but normal AFP may be at greater risk of being complicated later by poor growth (intra-uterine growth retardation, IUGR), by pregnancy-induced hypertension (high blood pressure; PIH) or by toxaemia of pregnancy (*see* Chapter 12). Therefore, should you choose to undergo full AFP screening, you may be able to obtain information that allows you to take steps either to prevent or to reduce the consequences of many potential complications.

You may, however, choose not to undergo any of the AFP screening tests, but wait until your child is born to discover if any abnormality exists and thus avoid the emotional burden that some women feel while awaiting the outcome of each level of more specific testing. It is also important to remember that, if your doctor suggests having further tests, he or she is not trying to put you through the emotional wringer, but is trying to gather the most information possible to enable you to have the healthiest possible baby. However, it is your *body*, and you should make the final decision about which tests are to be done.

Ultrasound

This is a widely available and extremely revealing antenatal testing device. It works by sending sound waves through the skin (or through the vagina in the case of vaginal ultrasound). Those waves are bounced back at different rates, depending on with what they come into contact – e.g. bone, fluid (blood, urine, etc.) or soft tissue(liver, lung, heart, etc.). Within the ultrasound machine is a computer that translates those differently reflected sound waves into a picture which is then displayed on a television-like screen. Ultrasound can also detect movement (the beating of the baby's heart, its breathing and the movement of its arms, legs, and body) by calculating the different reflections of sound waves over time and projecting them on the screen like a video image. This works on the same principle as the Doppler, the auditory ultrasonic machine; in this, the computer translates sound waves into an audible sound (such as your baby's heartbeat) instead of a picture.

Ultrasound is not an X-ray; no radiation is involved. It has been an integral part of obstetrical practice for more than 15 years and no harmful effects have been demonstrated whatsoever. Over these years, the ultrasound has become more and more sophisticated, the image that it can produce has become increasingly clear, and its place in obstetrics has become more and more widespread. It offers a non-invasive way of gathering information about a pregnancy, from three weeks after conception until the birth.

At the beginning of pregnancy, ultrasound can locate and outline the forming embryo. It can record whether the pregnancy is occurring inside of the uterus or whether it is an ectopic pregnancy (outside of the womb; *see* Chapter 12). If ultrasound is performed every five to ten days at the beginning of pregnancy, healthy growth can be documented; unhealthy growth which can lead to miscarriage can also be discovered. In addition, a multiple birth (twins, triplets, etc.) can be detected early, and the heartbeat of the baby – or babies – can be seen on ultrasound as early as seven weeks after your last period.

During the first 12 weeks of pregnancy, a skilled ultrasonographer (ultrasound operator) can accurately predict the length of the pregnancy (that is, the "gestational age" of the foetus), plus or minus three days. Between 12 and 19 weeks, the ultrasound is accurate in predicting gestational age to within five days. Because ultrasound can be so accurate in its ability to date a pregnancy (predict an accurate gestational age), the majority of women in Britain are offered an ultrasound scan at 16 weeks to assess the well-being of the baby and so that their "due date" can be accurately predicted. An accurate due date is extremely important because it allows pregnancies that turn out to be premature or overdue and pregnancies that are complicated by the mother's diabetes to be carefully monitored. Because ultrasound becomes less and less accurate in predicting gestational age as the pregnancy progresses past 20 weeks, the results of early ultrasound can't be replaced by doing the ultrasound later on.

However, as the pregnancy progresses further, ultrasound can reveal enormous amounts of other information. If the baby's growth rate begins to lag, a series of ultrasound scans can be undertaken to verify and record this intra-uterine growth retardation (IUGR). Ultrasound can visualize a baby's normal organs and it can document the absence of or abnormality in a foetal organ. It can show the baby's position – head down (vertex), bottom or feet down (breech), back down or up with the baby lying straight across (transverse) – and it can determine the location of the placenta. The weight of the baby may be estimated, but if the scan is done close to the birth, this estimate may be inaccurate by as much as 10–20 per cent. Ultrasound can also be used to estimate the amount of amniotic fluid which surrounds the baby: an overabundance may indicate a problem, and

An ultrasound scan can give a great deal of information about the baby's growth and well-being. You can see the scan yourself on the TV screen, and the operator will be able to help you interpret what you see.

a diminishing amount below a certain threshold may also be worrisome. The baby's activities may be observed with ultrasound. A healthy baby has a normal repertoire of activities – breathing, body and limb movements, blinking, clenching its fists, sucking its thumb, and playing with its umbilical cord and body parts.

Although ultrasound is an extremely useful diagnostic tool, you must remember that it is only a tool. It does not provide perfect information and it does not replace the knowledge and wisdom of the mother and of medical staff, and babies grow just as well without being watched on ultrasound. Should a problem arise, however, this technique can prove to be very helpful.

69

More sophisticated tests

Amniocentesis

Antenatal genetic testing is always offered to women whose babies are at risk of a genetic abnormality. Such testing, however, must not pose a greater risk to the pregnancy than would the abnormality that it is supposed to identify. In other words, the chances of finding an abnormality must exceed the risks of the test.

Amniocentesis is a well-established test used in antenatal screening. It is used to detect a number of genetic disorders, particularly Down's syndrome, because the risk of Down's syndrome progressively increases as mothers get older. Pregnant women of 35 and older are usually routinely offered amniocentesis.

Amniocentesis is generally performed at about 16 weeks, when an overall assessment of the baby by ultrasound can be made fairly accurately. The ultrasound can determine if there are any gross abnormalities, and can assess the placenta and amniotic fluid. The woman's belly is cleaned thoroughly and, using sterile technique, a very fine needle is inserted through it, straight through the uterine wall and the amniotic sac and into the amniotic fluid.

You may wonder why all this poses so little danger to the foetus, since the idea of putting a needle into the sac around the baby sounds so scary. However, by using ultrasound to guide the needle, a site may be chosen far from the foetus, and in any case, most babies seem automatically to get out of the way as the needle enters the sac. Once it is in place, the sharp central portion of the needle is removed, leaving the blunt outer sheath. Sometimes babies will come close to the sheath, and occasionally will even seem to play with it. (Remember that the sharp needle part has been removed.) Once the thin, straw-like sheath is in the sac, a small amount of amniotic fluid may be drawn out with a syringe and then sent to a laboratory for analysis. The sheath is then removed. The fluid is replaced by the foetus and placenta. You may feel a little uterine cramping afterwards, so it is advisable to take it easy for 24 hours after the test.

The risks of the procedure are really very low: in most major hospital centres, the risk of miscarrying soon after amniocentesis is less than 1 in 100. (Remember that about 5 per cent of all pregnancies miscarry after the first trimester; *see* Chapter 12.) Genetic testing is only ever suggested when the risk of carrying a foetus with a genetic defect is greater than 1 in 100.

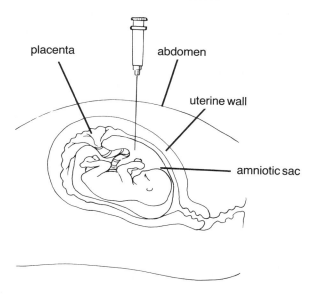

Amniocentesis. A needle contained within a very thin, straw-like sheath is inserted into the amniotic sac so that some of the fluid surrounding the baby can be collected for examination.

The results of the amniocentesis are usually ready in two to three weeks. These will not tell whether the baby is completely healthy. They will only answer the specific questions for which the test was devised. Does the baby have the normal number of chromosomes? Is the AFP in the amniotic fluid normal? Does the foetus carry the chromosome for Tay-Sachs (a serious disease of metabolism common among Ashkenazi Jews and French Canadians)? Does the baby's blood show signs of the inherited blood disorders sickle cell disease or thalassaemia? Is it a boy or a girl (whether a certain disease develops may depend on the sex)? In other words, testing the amniotic fluid around the baby reveals only specific answers, not whether the baby is healthy or not.

Amniocentesis may also be used late in pregnancy to test for substances secreted by the baby into the fluid which would indicate that its lungs are mature. These tests measure the lecithin/sphigomyelin (L/S) ratio and look for the presence of *phosphatidylglycerol* (pg). The presence of these substances in the amniotic fluid give almost certain assurance that the baby could be delivered safely early if need be without the risk of developing respiratory distress syndrome. Amniocentesis may also be used in the later stages of pregnancy if an infection around the baby is suspected. A sample of amniotic fluid would then be sent to the lab looking for an infective agent which can sometimes precipitate premature labour.

Chorionic villus sampling (CVS)

A more recent genetic screening test available at some major medical centres is *chorionic villus sampling* (CVS), sometimes called *chorion biopsy*. This procedure, performed at between 9 and 12 weeks, involves the removal of a tiny piece of the forming placenta (the *chorion*). This can be done in one of two ways: depending on which route provides the easiest access to the chorionic tissue, a sample is obtained either through the belly wall ("transabdominally") or through the vagina and then through the cervix ("transcervically"). If the transabdominal route is chosen, then the skin of the mother's belly is cleaned and prepared in a sterile manner as in amniocentesis. Because a larger-sized needle is required to remove chorionic tissue

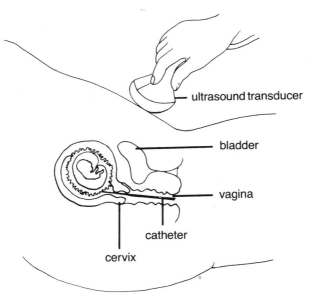

Chorionic villus sampling (CVS). Here, the sample is obtained through the vagina and cervix (transcervically). It can also be obtained through the belly wall (transabdominally).

than is required to remove amniotic fluid, a local anaesthetic is injected into the skin and into the underlying layers of tissue up to but not including the wall of the uterus. The needle is then inserted, under ultrasound guidance, along the path of the anaesthetic and into the uterus to the side of the placenta that the baby faces (the *chorionic villus*). Abdominal ultrasonic guidance is also employed when the transcervical approach is used. In this, the vagina and cervix are first cleaned with surgical soap, and then a very fine plastic tube (*catheter*) is inserted through the cervix to reach the chorionic villus. In either approach, a small sample of the chorion tissue is obtained and sent to a laboratory; the results are available in five days or less.

CVS has two advantages over amniocentesis – quicker results, available earlier in the pregnancy. However, the miscarriage rate after CVS is almost 10 per cent. (Remember that 17.5 per cent of *known* pregnancies are spontaneously miscarried in the first trimester.) Because CVS is carried out early in pregnancy, there will always be a higher rate of miscarriage following it (or any other invasive first trimester testing) than for amniocentesis, which is carried out when pregnancy is more established.

After genetic testing

If you have chosen to have genetic testing, what should you do if the results report something abnormal? Clearly this depends on many things, most importantly the nature of the abnormality and on the beliefs and feelings of you and your partner. If you have any problem understanding the results, ask your doctor or midwife or the genetics counsellor associated with the medical centre where the test was performed. Just because genetic screening has been offered to you does not mean that an abnormal result should lead to abortion. Genetic screening, like all antenatal testing, is meant to offer information. It should help you and your partner make informed decisions that should lead to the best possible outcome for your pregnancy in the circumstances.

Glucose tolerance test (GTT)

As you enter the last third of your pregnancy, a new balance is reached between you and your baby. Your baby will be adding muscle and fat, and your hormones will reach a balance to sustain the baby's growth. These demands put all pregnant women at risk of "diabetes of pregnancy" (*gestational diabetes*). It is for this reason that your doctor or midwife may suggest that you be tested for diabetes sometime between 24 and 28 weeks of pregnancy. If you agree, you will first be asked to drink a very sweet liquid (which contains exactly 50 grams of glucose), wait one hour and then have a blood sample drawn, which is tested for blood sugar level. If it is above a specified value, then you are a candidate for the more complex three-hour test. As previously noted, a raised level of blood sugar on the initial one-hour screening test does *not* mean that you are diabetic.

The three-hour test requires that you fast from midnight of the night before. (Your doctor or midwife may suggest that, for the two days prior to the test, you eat a diet rich in complex carbohydrates, such as bread, rice, pasta, potatoes and cereals.) Your blood will be drawn as soon as you arrive at the hospital in the morning so that a fasting blood sugar level will be obtained. Then you will be given a bottle or glass of a very sweet liquid (containing exactly 100 grams of glucose). After you drink this, blood samples will be taken from you at one-, two- and at three-hour intervals. If either the fasting blood sugar level is raised or *any* two values are, then you are, by definition, a gestational diabetic. This does not mean that you will have diabetes for the rest of your life. It means that, during this pregnancy, you must follow a special diet and may require insulin injections during the last third of your pregnancy. About 15 per cent of pregnant women tested will show abnormal results in their one-hour screening test, and approximately 3–5 per cent of those will have abnormal results on the three-hour test. This means that those 3–5 per cent have gestational diabetes.

Maintaining very tightly controlled blood sugar levels is essential in pregnancy. If there is a lot of sugar in your blood, some of it will cross the placenta to the baby, and the baby will metabolize the sugar and store it as fat. This is why babies of mothers with uncontrolled diabetes, tend to be large. In addition, diabetes tends to put extra stress on small blood vessels, and in pregnancy one of the organs full of small blood vessels is the placenta. If the placenta comes under stress, it may age more quickly. And as your pregnancy progresses closer to delivery, a placenta which has been stressed may not have as much in reserve and may not nourish your baby adequately. For this reason, your doctor may choose to institute tests for foetal well-being (*see below*) as your pregnancy draws to a close.

Most women who have gestational diabetes will have no further blood sugar problems after childbirth. However, they are at greater risk of developing diabetes with subsequent pregnancies, and much later in life or if they become seriously obese (*see also* Chapter 11).

Other tests

As you enter your third trimester, your blood count may be checked for anaemia, and the syphilis test may also be repeated.

Foetal well-being tests

As your pregnancy approaches delivery time, how will you know if all is well inside? There is no window in the womb, no zip that allows easy access to the baby.

If your pregnancy has been uneventful, and no medical problems develop in the final weeks, then no special tests need be performed. Just because a multitude of hi-tech tests are available doesn't mean that you must or should be subjected to them. If you and your baby seem entirely healthy, you don't need them. If however, your pregnancy has been complicated by medical problems (such as diabetes or high blood pressure), or if you go more than ten days past your due date (when the placenta may be getting too old to sustain the foetus effectively), or if your baby does not seem to be growing adequately, then you will most likely be a candidate for the various available tests of your baby's health – foetal well-being tests. These include the non-stress test, the stress test and the biophysical profile. PUBS (percutaneous umbilical blood sampling) is a very new test in which a sample of the baby's blood is obtained and sent for testing.

The non-stress test (NST)

This involves a continuous ultrasound evaluation of the baby's heartbeat over a period of 20–45 minutes, while, at the same time, the mother notes each time the baby moves. In general, with each foetal movement, there is a rise in the foetal heartbeat, much the same as when your heart rate goes up with increased physical activity, even if that activity is modest (like climbing a few stairs). If the foetal heart rate remains constant, it may only mean that the baby is napping, and in that case, the test is continued until the baby wakes up. If a sleep pattern continues (even after the mother is given fruit juice or coffee) or if the baby's heartbeat goes down during the test, then further testing is required. If the baby appears healthy during the non-stress test, is it possible to predict how long the baby will remain healthy? While a baby who appears healthy on the non-stress test will probably remain healthy for at least 72 hours, there is no guarantee. No foetal well-being test is absolutely accurate.

The biophysical profile
The biophysical profile is a visual ultrasound evaluation of the baby's activities and the quantity of amniotic fluid surrounding it. This is done in conjunction with a non-stress test and is used to add more information to the NST and hopefully make it more possible to predict the baby's health over the next few days. Some medical centres give a score from 0 to 10; a score of 7 or more is acceptable. Other medical centres give an unscored overall foetal evaluation.

The stress test
If the NST and/or the biophysical profile indicate that the baby's health may not be optimal, then a stress test may be needed. This is designed to create uterine contractions – a sort of mini dry-run of labour – in an effort to evaluate how the baby would respond if put under the stress of real labour. Uterine contractions are created in one of two ways: either by having the mother stimulate her nipples (nipple stimulation test), thus releasing her own natural uterus-contracting hormone *oxytocin*; or by the administration of small but ever-increasing doses of oxytocin intravenously. Either way, enough oxytocin is released or administered until the uterus contracts a specified number of times in a specified number of minutes. A healthy baby's heartbeat need not rise, but it should not drop when it is being challenged by the stress of contractions.

Percutaneous umbilical blood sampling (PUBS)
PUBS is an extremely new test designed to obtain a direct blood sample from the baby. The mother's belly is first cleaned with surgical soap. Then, using ultrasound as a guide, a loop of the baby's umbilical cord (usually near the site where the cord inserts into the placenta) is located. Using the same technique described for amniocentesis, a very fine needle is inserted into the mother's belly and then through the uterine wall, but in this case, the needle goes directly into the vein within the umbilical cord. A sample of the baby's blood is

taken which can be used for a variety of tests to evaluate foetal well-being.

All of these foetal well-being tests try to measure how much reserve the baby and placenta have in an effort to predict how much longer the baby should remain in the womb. (Remember, these tests are only performed when an obstetrical or medical problem is complicating the pregnancy.) If the tests indicate that the uterine environment is not optimal, then delivery should be planned, either by inducing labour or performing a Caesarean section.

No test will be able to make sure the baby is "fine"; no test can guarantee that you will have a healthy baby. But they will give information that may enable you and your doctor and midwife to devise a plan that will lead to the healthiest possible outcome. Ultimately, you are the one to decide which tests you choose to undergo. You may need only a few basic ones or you may require intensive antenatal testing. In the future, there may be many different ways to evaluate your unborn baby's health, but no matter how simple or how sophisticated the tests may be, they will always be designed to promote your baby's well-being.

PART II

Health Care During Pregnancy

CHAPTER FIVE

Exercise in Pregnancy

Exercise should be considered an integral part of everyone's lifestyle. Carrying out a balanced exercise regime will do much to promote your physical well-being, and this is especially true in pregnancy. Exercise improves your circulation, increases your lung capacity, strengthens your heart, tones your muscles, and generally makes you feel better.

Exercise is essentially movement. It may range from subtle stretching to vigorous aerobic workouts. It should be stressed emphatically, though, that it is not necessary to join an expensive health club or invest in videos or stationary bicycles to get some exercise. Before the myriad of home appliances became available, people had no trouble getting exercise through the basic activities of daily living. Imagine the work involved in washing the family laundry by hand – that alone is equivalent to a workout on a sophisticated exercise machine. And hanging laundry on a clothes-line is equal to a stretching workout. Chopping wood, beating rugs, picking fruit, walking to the nearest village or town are all activities that exercised diverse groups of muscles. Although, in modern times, it is not necessary to do these things to survive, many people do some of them at least to some extent, and as a result, they are probably getting more exercise than they think. If you do lead a fairly sedentary life, this may be the time to start *moving* more. Pregnancy is a good time to examine your lifestyle, and make it as healthy as possible.

Exercise, to some degree, is recommended in pregnancy. Aside from the benefits listed above, exercise allows you to become more in tune with your body, and increases your awareness of individual muscle groups. This will help you throughout your pregnancy and labour, because you will be able to relax certain muscles at will. Relaxation is crucial during pregnancy and labour. Exercise helps you to achieve this.

Everyday activities

A great exercise during pregnancy is walking. If done at a brisk pace, it increases your heart rate and tones your leg muscles. It can also be done with your family or friends, allowing you time to visit. You may want to combine walking with errands if you live close enough to the shops. Try to avoid hopping in the car every time you need to go a short distance.

As far as other general activities go, as long as you don't go in for any rash physical feats, are well nourished and have no medical problems, you can live a normal life while pregnant. Remember, pregnancy is not an illness. It is a normal life process, and you can continue with activities to which you are accustomed, including jogging, cycling and aerobics. The key is to use your common sense and listen to what your body is telling you. If you are tired and don't feel up to a 20-mile cycling trip, don't go or only go a part of the way. Rest when you feel the need. But if you're feeling great and look forward to these activities, by all means do what you feel like doing. As your pregnancy progresses, you will probably feel the need to slow down somewhat. Give in to that need, and rest more often.

Pregnancy is probably not the time to start doing very strenuous activities to which you are not accustomed. However, walking, stretching, swimming and cycling are all exercises you could begin while pregnant, as long as you build up slowly. Swimming is especially recommended because the buoyancy of the water protects you from straining any muscles. Many health clubs and local sports centres have exercise classes for pregnant women. The instructors should be aware of your individual needs and level of competency.

Are there limitations to exercising while pregnant?
Most activities in pregnancy are acceptable, if you were accustomed to them before you became pregnant. However, there are some exceptions. High-impact sports (such as rugby, lacrosse, skydiving) are to be avoided in pregnancy; the sudden, intense jarring may cause the placenta to separate from the wall of the uterus, which can have

serious consequences. Scuba diving is also not recommended during pregnancy because the sudden changes in pressure could be harmful to your baby. High-altitude activities may also be a problem. There is not as much oxygen at high altitudes, and the oxygen supply to the foetus may be compromised. This is especially true for women who, from their usual low-altitude habitat, travel to a high-altitude site in order to engage in a sport such as skiing or hiking.

Specific exercises

In addition to just moving more in general, the following exercises may be helpful in toning and stretching your muscles. They may also help to alleviate the minor aches and pains of pregnancy.

Proper standing posture
Keep your head raised to align the rest of your body. Shoulders are straight and your bottom is tucked in.

Proper sitting posture
Maintain proper body alignment while sitting. This will prevent lower backache and alleviate the shortness of breath associated with the latter part of pregnancy.

Lifting position
To lift anything, use your leg muscles instead of your back muscles. Lower yourself down to the appropriate level in a squatting motion, and keep your back straight while lifting. You will feel the muscles in your legs as you rise to a standing position.

Pelvic rock
This is an important exercise if you suffer from sciatica or lower backache. It strengthens your pelvic area, and may also be of help in turning the baby if it is in the breech position. Go on to your hands and knees, with your hands directly under your shoulders. Your back should be flat not sagging. Take a deep breath and, as you exhale, hump your back like a cat. You should tighten your abdominal and buttock muscles as you do this. Hold this position for a count of three, then relax. Repeat 8–10 times.

EXERCISE IN PREGNANCY

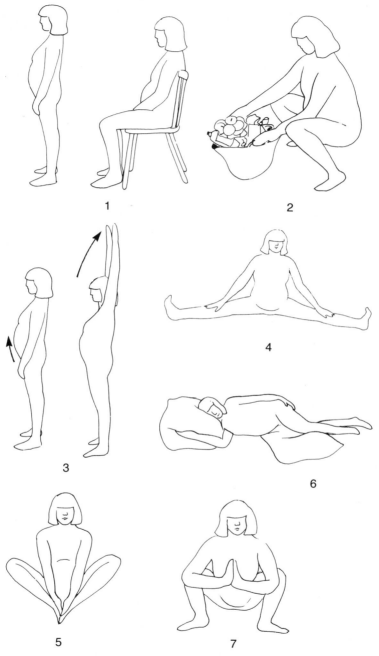

(1) The correct way to stand and sit. (2) The correct way to lift anything. (3) Arm stretching. (4) Leg stretching. (5) The tailor position. (6) Lying on one side, supported with pillows. (7) Squatting.

Arm stretching

Stretching is a good way to relieve tension; arm-stretching exercises will also help to relieve upper backache. Stand tall with your arms extended out at the sides. Slowly raise your arms until they are straight up over your head. Slowly lower them down to your sides. Repeat 6–7 times, breathing slowly and deeply. This exercise may also be done while lying on the floor.

Leg stretching

Sit on the floor with your legs apart and your back straight. Raise your arms over your head and reach towards your ankles. Stretch only as far as you comfortably can. Do not push this to the point of pain. This not only stretches your leg muscles, but your arms and back as well. You may also lie on your back and raise and stretch one leg at a time. Do not try to lift both legs at once, as this exerts too much strain on your abdominal muscles.

Tailor position

Sit on the floor with your back straight. Bend your knees and cross your legs at the ankles. This position will relax your pelvic area, and should be used often when just sitting.

Side-lying with pillows

You should practise being totally relaxed, and this is a good position for this. The weight of the baby is off your major blood vessels, your upper leg and head are supported with pillows. Concentrate on relaxing every muscle in your body, working from your toes, feet, calves, etc., up to your neck and head.

Squatting

Squatting opens up your pelvis to its widest dimension. Many women would like to push their babies out in this position, but their legs tire too easily. Practising this position while pregnant will help to strengthen your thigh muscles, and allow you to squat for longer periods during labour. Be sure to stand up slowly from a squatting position to prevent lightheadedness.

Pelvic-floor exercises

Important exercises for every woman, pregnant or not, are pelvic-floor exercises – that is, tightening and relaxing the pelvic-floor muscles, which are the ones you use to stop and start the flow of urine. Hold these muscles tight to a count of 10, then relax them to a count of 5. Perform these tightenings and relaxings 10 times.

These exercises will tone up the muscles in this area, and will help prevent complications resulting from poor pelvic tone later in life, such as urinary incontinence. They also promote circulation to this area, facilitating healing after childbirth, and allow you to relax them more readily during delivery. Try to do them 80 to 100 times a day – every day. You can remind yourself to do them by associating them with certain daily events, such as waiting at a lift or at traffic lights, or when the phone rings.

CHAPTER SIX

Nutrition in Pregnancy

Pregnancy, more than any other time in your life, is a time to reflect upon your lifestyle and habits. If you smoke, drink heavily or take "recreational" drugs, concern for your unborn child may provide enough impetus to abandon these unhealthy habits. The same is true for your nutritional status. If you have only coffee in the morning, a bar of chocolate for lunch and crisps for dinner, pregnancy is the time to start some good dietary habits which will hopefully last a lifetime. Pregnancy is a great way of making you eager to learn about your body in a way you never thought possible.

There are mountains of information available to pregnant women about nutrition. There are many different theories on how much weight you *should* gain, which foods *will* harm the baby, how much milk you *have* to drink, how many grams of protein you *must* eat – in fact, there are so many theories that you need a PhD just to make lunch. In that sort of atmosphere, mealtimes just aren't enjoyable. Granted, pregnant women should take a bit more care about what they eat, but what that is is not that much different from the well-balanced diet everyone should be eating.

People don't eat food *groups* – they eat food. They also don't eat *milligrams* and *grams* of food – they eat servings. And people don't *eat* vitamins – they eat foods which contain vitamins. Pregnant women tend to get caught up in the frenzy of analysing everything which enters their mouths. They either feel they have fulfilled the obligatory requirement, or they are riddled with guilt for eating something that isn't "allowed" on their diet. Yes, there are nutritional requirements in pregnancy, and these will be discussed with examples of foods which contain them. However, when learning about nutrition, remember that *anything* in excess is bad for you. This includes alcohol, sweets and even vitamin pills. Anything can be toxic to your baby if taken to an extreme, while most things in moderation are OK.

Weight gain

One of the first things that women want to know when they are pregnant is "How much weight should I gain?" There is no magic number to answer this question. Women start out at different weights, and heavy women need to put on less weight than very thin women. Teenagers need to gain more than older women to fulfil their own dietary requirements as they are still developing themselves. So the recommended weight gain varies from about 22 to 34 lb (10–15 kg), depending on your age and pre-pregnant weight. Below, a weight gain of 24 $\frac{3}{4}$ lb (11.2 kg) has been broken down to show you approximately where it all goes.

Placenta	1$\frac{1}{4}$ lb (0.55 kg)
Uterus	2 lb (0.90 kg)
Baby	7$\frac{1}{2}$ lb (3.40 kg) (average)
Amniotic fluid	1$\frac{1}{2}$ lb (0.70 kg)
Blood	4 lb (1.80 kg)
Breasts	1 lb (0.45 kg)
Tissue fluid	2$\frac{1}{2}$ lb (1.15 kg)
Fat stores	5 lb (2.25 kg)

Pregnancy is a time for eating a well-balanced diet, containing a wide variety of foods. The variety will assure you of getting all the nutrients you need. You should never try to lose weight during pregnancy. This should be done either before you become pregnant, or after the baby is born. If you are overweight and usually binge on sweets and fattening foods, by all means cut those out. But they should be replaced with nutritious snacks and meals instead.

Many women worry that they are gaining too much weight during their pregnancy. However, everyone has a different metabolic rate, and some women gain more weight than others even if they are all eating the same amount.

If you feel that you are gaining too much weight, write down everything you eat for a whole week. This includes what you drink and how much. Then examine your list. You may find that you had forgotten about the small snacks you munched now and then, all of which can add up to a lot of empty calories. Putting everything down on paper will show you which of the things you can cut out of your diet. You should not cut out the foods with nutritious value; however, if you are eating them in exceedingly large quantities, you might cut these down.

Some women, if they are very nauseated, do lose weight during the first trimester. However, while this is not an ideal situation, the unborn baby should not suffer: it usually takes what it needs first, and then the expectant mother's nutritional needs are met. Calcium is an example of one of these nutritional needs. You can produce a bouncing baby, full term, well developed and healthy, even if you did not receive enough calcium during the pregnancy. Your own teeth and bones will supply that calcium, thus depleting their strength.

Dietary needs during pregnancy

Protein
This is essential for the tissue development of every aspect of your developing baby, from the brain to the fingernails. Since your baby is continually developing throughout the pregnancy, your protein needs are quite high, and you require even more if you are a teenager and still growing yourself. Sources of protein are meat, fish, poultry, eggs, dairy products, peanut butter, pulses (beans, lentils, etc.), tofu (soya-bean curd), nuts and whole grains.

You should include protein in every meal and snack in some fashion. If you are eating the traditional three meals a day, you should supplement these with two protein snacks so that you eat at least five protein servings a day; if you are eating small frequent meals, you should ensure that you get this amount of protein. Again, variety is the key. If you don't like eggs in the morning, whole-grain cereal with milk is a fine protein source, or whole-grain toast with peanut butter. In general, the meats and dairy products that are lower in fat are higher in protein. Also, the harder the cheese is, the lower its fat content and the higher its protein content. Refined foods such as white bread should be removed from your diet. For the same amount of calories, whole-grain breads offer you much more nutritional value. Cheese and biscuits make a good snack; this provides both protein and calcium. Suggested menus, snacks and recipes are listed at the end of this chapter.

Calcium

This is essential in any woman's diet, regardless of age and pregnancy. Calcium is the main component of bones and teeth and a constant supply is needed throughout life, not only when the bones and teeth are forming. A lack of calcium can cause brittle bones and allow the teeth to decay more easily. While a foetus is developing, the calcium demand is great. If the dietary needs are not met, the baby will take what calcium it needs from the mother, depleting her own stores so that she does not meet her own bodily needs.

In pregnancy, daily calcium needs could be met by drinking 2 pints (1.1 litres) of milk per day (and skimmed milk contains a little more calcium than whole milk). However, many women ask if they have to drink so much milk a day, because they don't like milk; they find this requirement overwhelming. The answer is no. Milk is not the only source of calcium: all dairy products contain calcium as well as varying amounts of protein, and you should eat a variety. Cheese, yoghurt, cottage cheese, ice cream, ice milk and frozen yoghurt all contain calcium, and they should be incorporated into your diet. If you have milk on your cereal in the morning, cheese on your sandwich at lunch, a yoghurt for an afternoon snack and a hot chocolate in the evening, you've got your four servings – simple. Having a glass of milk with either lunch or dinner or both would be great, but you don't have to. If you love to drink lots of milk and eat cheese at every opportunity, that's fine, too: it's very difficult to take in too much calcium during pregnancy.

Additional ways of getting calcium into your diet include: adding dry milk powder to the things that you bake; adding cottage cheese to scrambled eggs; making creamy salad dressings with plain yoghurt; and sprinkling Parmesan cheese on salads or popcorn.

There are sources of calcium which are not part of the dairy group, and by eating them, women who are allergic to dairy products can still get enough calcium in their diet without the need for calcium supplements. These foods include: fish that are canned with the bones, such as sardines or herring: soyabeans, tofu, almonds, sesame seeds and sesame paste (tahini), and dark green vegetables. If you eat four servings of these foods a day, your calcium needs will be met.

Some people lack the enzyme *lactase*, which allows milk to be digested. For lactose-intolerant women, there is milk which contains lactase supplements. You can also buy lactase supplement tablets, which can be taken before meals containing milk.

Iron

The need for iron in pregnancy is almost as great as the need for calcium. Iron is essential for your blood to carry oxygen to your tissues efficiently. A lack of iron is manifested most often by fatigue. This is common even in women who are not pregnant, simply because you lose blood every month during your period. When a foetus is demanding some of your iron stores, the fatigue can become overwhelming. Your iron level will be checked periodically during the pregnancy, and iron supplements are sometimes routinely pre-scribed just to make sure women get as much as they need. These supplements are not without their side-effects, however – primarily constipation. Iron is better absorbed from the food in your diet, and the iron you take in with food will also not be as constipating as the pills. The absorption of iron is enhanced by vitamin C or acidic foods, so try to bear that in mind when planning your diet. Iron is inhibited by calcium, so while taking an iron pill with a glass of milk is not harmful, it's just counterproductive.

Foods that are high in iron content include: red meat, especially organ meats such as liver and kidney; dried fruits such as apricots, prunes and raisins (and the juice of these fruits); black treacle; dark green vegetables such as broccoli, spinach, kale and collards; grains such as wheat germ or dried pulses. You should get as much of these foods into your diet as possible. Snack on dried fruits (especially if you are craving something sweet, as they are also high in sugar), include a dark green vegetable in your dinner every night, and try black treacle on a piece of toast or on top of cooked cereal. You also should do more cooking in a cast iron frying pan, as food (especially acidic ones) will absorb some of the iron from the pan. This really works and it's simple.

Vitamins

You can easily take in all the vitamins you require by eating a variety of fruits and vegetables and grains. It is not necessary to take special vitamins to produce a healthy baby, even though many doctors and midwives recommend them – and even scold women for not taking them – just to be sure that dietary needs are met. However, like iron, vitamins are best absorbed and utilized by the body when they are present in the food you eat.

Vitamin supplements can increase the nausea associated with the first trimester, and make food you should be eating even more unappealing. Even if you are getting all the nutrients you need through your diet, taking a vitamin supplement won't hurt you. Any excess of water-soluble vitamins such as B and C will leave your body through the urine once your daily needs have been met. While it is possible to overdose on fat-soluble vitamins A and D, the amount in any prescribed vitamin supplement won't hurt you, but taking additional vitamins may. Megadoses of vitamins can be *harmful*. The general rule is that you should not take any vitamins in addition to those prescribed for you – and if your diet is a good, well-balanced one, you don't even require those.

Vitamin A is a fat-soluble vitamin and can be stored in your fatty tissues. It is an important nutrient during the first trimester when the foetus is developing so rapidly. It is best obtained from dairy products, liver, yellow and orange vegetables, green leafy vegetables, apricots, cantaloupe melon and cooked prunes.

The *B vitamins* (which actually include 11 different vitamins) are the key vitamins in nervous system and skin development. They are most plentiful in whole grains such as brown rice, wheat germ, rolled oats, bulgar wheat, cracked wheat, bran and millet. They are also found in meats (especially organ meats), milk, dark green vegetables, fresh fruits and nuts. You can see that a wide variety of foods is needed to give you an adequate daily supply of these vitamins. Four or more servings of whole grains per day is recommended to meet your needs.

Vitamin C, like the B vitamins, is water soluble, which means that your body does not store it. As a result, you need a source of this vitamin every day. Vitamin C is destroyed by heat, so fresh fruits are your best source. Citrus fruits such as oranges, lemons, grapefruit and limes contain large amounts of vitamin C. Other fruits, such as cantaloupe melon, strawberries and tomatoes are also good sources. This vitamin plays a strong part in the development of healthy skin, hair and teeth. Healthy blood vessels and muscles are also dependent upon this vitamin. An adequate amount of vitamin C can prevent illness and promote healing.

Vitamin D, necessary for the absorption of calcium to promote strong bones and teeth, can be found in milk, fish and green leafy vegetables. Vitamin D is also produced by the body when bare skin is exposed to sunlight (even when you use a sun-screen cream).

The other vitamins (E and K) and minerals (e.g. zinc, magnesium) are needed in the body in small amounts. They are present in the foods mentioned above, and a well-balanced diet will provide all that you need.

Carbohydrates

Carbohydrates, or energy foods, are also important in pregnancy. There are two types. Refined carbohydrates include white bread, white sugar and all the other different names for sugar, which simply provide "empty calories", or calories that give you no nutrition. These types of carbohydrates should be reduced severely during pregnancy. This is not true of the other category of carbohydrates, which include all the foods that provide nutrients and fibre (roughage). Breads, pasta, rice and cereals of the whole-grain variety offer you not only energy, but lots of protein, B vitamins and roughage as well.

Since everyone craves sweets now and then, you should make your own, and make them as nutritious as possible. Oatmeal biscuits with raisins and nuts are not only good, but good for you. If you make them yourself, you can control how much sugar goes in. You can also add such things as black treacle or wheat germ to get a few extra nutrients (*see recipes*). These are also great treats for children, so practise now.

Fluids

Another important factor in a healthy diet is fluid. Many women and children do not drink enough throughout the day. Lack of fluid is the biggest cause of constipation. Fluids aid digestion, flush the urinary tract, promote good skin tone, and help prevent bacteria and viruses from developing into infections. All women should drink six to eight glasses of fluids per day, and this is especially important if you are pregnant. With the growing uterus resting on your bladder and leaving less space for the urine to flow, drinking lots of fluids prevents urinary tract infections which are common in pregnancy. Fluids also play a big part in controlling the high blood pressure associated with pre-eclampsia (*see* Chapter 12).

Water is an excellent drink, and three of your glasses a day should be water. It gives you the fluids you need with no calories. Milk or fruit juices are also good to drink, and will give you some calcium and vitamins as well. Try to avoid taking coffee or regular tea to fulfil your fluid needs, as the caffeine they contain is not recommended in large amounts (*see below*). Herbal teas are fine, and some are thought to be soothing to the nerves and digestive tract (chamomile, and peppermint especially). The occasional soft drink will not hurt you, and may settle your stomach if you are nauseated, but they should never be used to meet your fluid needs. They contain far too much sugar and salt, and diet drinks contain chemicals which may be harmful to the foetus if taken in large quantities (*see below*). Pregnancy is not the time to eat or drink large amounts of "diet" *anything*.

Vegetarian diets

If you are a vegetarian, you will have to examine your diet carefully during pregnancy. It is possible to get all the nutrients you need without eating meat, fish or poultry. This, however, will take a good bit of research and planning. Your protein intake will need to be assessed daily, and you will need a combination of grains or a combination of grains with dairy products. If you eat no dairy products as well as no meat, it is going to be more difficult (though not impossible) to take in your daily requirements. This type of diet should be done knowledgeably even when you are not pregnant. Many vegetarians who abstain from dairy products will eat them while pregnant.

There are many good books which are full of information on vegetarian diets.

Foods to avoid in pregnancy

Technology, in an attempt to make our lives easier and improve our quality of living, has done some remarkable things to the food we eat. Meat doesn't spoil as rapidly, neither do bread and cereals. Fattening foods are produced with artificial sweeteners so people can have what they like without the calories. Foods are refined and packaged for easy, quick preparation. Unfortunately, all these wonders of modern times have not really done us much good in promoting a nutritious lifestyle. This is especially true during pregnancy. Many of the additives and preservatives found in packaged foods may be harmful to a developing foetus. This is particularly worrisome in the case of aspartame, marketed under the brand name "NutraSweet". Some research suggests that, if taken in large amounts, this substance may adversely affect a foetus. For this reason, diet foods and especially diet soft drinks should be avoided.

Foods high in preservatives, such as highly processed meats containing nitrates and nitrites, are also best avoided in large quantities. The research that has been done on laboratory animals shows some evidence that cancer and birth defects may be caused by high doses of these chemicals.

In recent years, caffeine has also been studied intensively, and very high doses have been associated with birth defects. Since caffeine is highly addictive, many women have a hard time giving up their morning tea or coffee. Your body does become accustomed to the kick it gets from caffeine. But after living without it for a while, your body adjusts, and you can be wide awake and function without it. Try to limit your caffeine intake to one cup a day.

Alcohol is another beverage which is known to be harmful to the foetus in large amounts (*see* Chapter 8).

Once a substance is known to affect an unborn child adversely in some way, it is usually portrayed as being absolutely, totally forbidden to pregnant women, and women who succumb to temptation need to wallow in guilt until they can see for themselves that their babies are all right. As always common sense is the key. The *occasional* use of a sugar substitute or the *occasional* eating of a slice of ham or salami is not going to produce a damaged baby. An *occasional* glass of wine or beer may help you to relax, and actually offer some beneficial effects. Likewise, the use of moderate amounts of alcohol while cooking will not be harmful. But drinking wine or beer every night, or going on a drunken binge is definitely harmful.

Sample menus

The following menus are suggestions for a balanced daily diet in pregnancy. They are only suggestions, and may certainly be adapted to accommodate likes, dislikes and cultural and ethnic variations.

Breakfast
- Bran cereal with banana and milk, decaffeinated coffee or tea

- Poached egg on whole-wheat toast, orange (fruit or juice), decaffeinated coffee or tea
- Oatmeal with milk and black treacle, juice or fruit, decaffeinated coffee or tea

Lunch
- Tuna sandwich with cheese, spinach salad, milk or juice
- Chef's salad (lettuce, chicken, cheese, tomato, hard-boiled eggs) with whole-wheat bread, milk
- Pizza with cheese and mince, salad, milk or juice

Dinner
- Meat, fish or poultry, baked potato, steamed broccoli, salad, milk
- Pasta with tomato and meat sauce, salad with raw spinach or broccoli
- Stir-fried beef or chicken with fresh vegetables, brown rice with sesame seeds

Snacks
Two snacks should be included in your diet each day, one mid-morning, and one in the late afternoon. These snacks should balance out the meals you eat, and help to fulfil your daily needs.
- Raw fruits or vegetables
- Dried apricots or prunes
- Toast with peanut butter and black treacle
- Bran muffins or other whole-grain muffins
- Cheese (cottage or hard) on biscuits or with an apple or pear
- Yoghurt, plain or add fruit and wheat germ
- Sardines on cream crackers
- Oatmeal biscuits

Recipes
The following basic recipes have been included to give you some ideas when planning a basic healthy diet. Remember that, when you make food from scratch, you have control over what goes into it, and can get the most nutrients for the calories. You can also be sure that there are no preservatives in it, and it's cheaper. These are just a

start. Look through your own cookbooks, and have fun planning and preparing a more nutritious diet for everyone.

Bran muffins

8 oz (225 g) whole-wheat flour
6 oz (175 g) wheat bran
1¼ tsp bicarbonate of soda
½ tsp cinnamon
½ tsp nutmeg
4 fl oz (125 ml) black treacle
8 fl oz (225 ml) milk

8 fl oz (225 ml) plain yoghurt
1 egg, beaten
2 tbsp (30 ml) oil
6 oz (175 g) raisins
1 apple, chopped
1 oz (25 g) chopped nuts

Preheat oven to 350°F (180°C, gas mark 4).
Mix dry ingredients together. In a separate bowl, mix black treacle, milk, yoghurt, egg and oil. Stir into dry ingredients, stirring just enough to moisten. Fold in raisins, apple and nuts. Pour into greased bun tins, and bake for 25 minutes.

Whole-wheat bread

16 fl oz (425 ml) milk
2 tbsp (30 ml) margarine
3 tsp dry yeast
4 fl oz (125 ml) black treacle

2 tbsp (30 ml) honey
4 oz (100 g) white flour
1¼–1½ lb (550–650 g)
whole-wheat flour

Preheat oven to 350°F (180°C, gas mark 4). Scald milk, and stir in margarine until melted. Cool until lukewarm, and then stir in yeast until dissolved. Add black treacle and honey. Mix the white flour with 1¼ lb (550 g) of the whole-wheat flour and beat into milk mixture 4 oz (100 g) at a time until a stiff dough forms; this may require adding another ¼ lb (100 g) whole-wheat flour. Turn out on to a floured surface and knead for about 10 minutes. Place in a greased bowl and turn the dough to grease the top. Cover with a damp towel and let rise for about 2 hours. Punch the dough down and knead again for about 10 minutes. Form into two loaves and place in greased loaf pans. Let rise until doubled. Brush the tops with milk, and bake in preheated oven for 45–50 minutes.

Creamy salad dressing

8 fl oz (225 ml) mayonnaise
1 tbsp chopped onion
1 tbsp chopped chives
1 to 2 garlic cloves, minced
¼ tsp black pepper
2 fl oz (50 ml) vinegar

8 fl oz (225 ml) plain yoghurt
1 tbsp chopped parsley
1 tbsp chopped basil
½ tsp salt
1 tbsp sugar
dash of Tabasco sauce

Blend all ingredients thoroughly. Use on salads or as a dip for vegetables.

Salad dressing with tahini

4 fl oz (125 ml) tahini (sesame paste)
4 fl oz (125 ml) olive oil
1 tbsp sugar
1 tbsp dried basil
$\frac{1}{4}$ tsp black pepper
1 tsp salt

4 fl oz (125 ml) herbed vinegar
(e.g. tarragon vinegar)
1 tbsp garlic powder *or* 2 garlic
cloves, minced
1 tbsp dried parsley
1 tsp Tabasco sauce

Mix all ingredients thoroughly. Let sit (covered) at room temperature for several hours to blend spices. Serve on salads.

"Soured cream" salad dressing

2 fl oz (50 ml) buttermilk
6 fl oz (175 ml) cottage cheese
3–5 spring onions

1 garlic clove
$\frac{1}{4}$ tsp vinegar
salt and pepper to taste

Blend all of the ingredients in a blender or food processor.

Sesame chicken

2 lb (900 g) chicken parts
1$\frac{1}{2}$ tbsp melted butter
salt and pepper to taste

juice of an orange
sesame seeds

Preheat oven to 350°F (180°C, gas mark 4). Coat the chicken lightly in butter. Season with salt and pepper. Place skin side down in baking dish. Squeeze $\frac{1}{2}$ of orange juice over chicken and then cover with sesame seeds. Bake approximately 20 minutes, then turn over the chicken pieces. Squeeze the other half of the orange juice over them and coat with sesame seeds again. Bake until brown and done.

Chicken soup

chicken parts (about 2 lb/900 g)
1 medium onion (with skin), quartered
1 carrot
1 stalk celery

salt and pepper to taste
4 sprigs parsley
1 tsp fresh dill or $\frac{1}{2}$ tsp dried dill
water to cover

Bring the ingredients to a boil and skim the grey froth from the top. Allow to simmer for an hour. Strain to make clear broth.

Variation 1: Egg-drop soup
Bring the broth to a vigorous boil and then stir in two beaten eggs.

Variation 2: Egg-ribbon soup
Beat two eggs and add a tablespoon of grated Parmesan cheese. Stir this into the vigorously boiling broth. Garnish with a little chopped parsley.

Variation 3: Chicken soup with Chinese vegetables

Add sliced mushrooms and carrots to boiling broth. Then add diced tofu. Then add mange-tout and a dash of soya sauce. Egg drop (*see above*) may also be added. At the last moment, spinach may also be added.

Basic fish recipe

Fillet of fish (sole, cod, plaice
  salmon, etc.)
1 tbsp white wine
juice of $\frac{1}{4}$ lemon or lime
$\frac{1}{3}$ stalk celery, finely chopped

salt and pepper to taste
fresh or dried herbs
  (liberal amount)
1 tsp minced spring onion or
  shallot

This dish may be either baked in the oven at 350°F (180°C, gas mark 4) or cooked in the microwave on high; the timing will depend on the type and thickness of the fish and, if cooking in a microwave, on the wattage. Just cover the fish with all the other ingredients.

Oatmeal biscuits

6 oz (175 g) butter
6 oz (175 g) brown sugar
1 egg
2 fl oz (50 ml) water
2 fl oz (50 ml) black treacle
1 tsp vanilla
4 oz (100 g) whole-wheat flour

$\frac{1}{2}$ tsp soda
8 oz (225 g) raisins
12 oz (350 g) rolled oats
1 tsp cinnamon
$\frac{1}{2}$ tsp cloves
2 oz (50 g) chopped nuts
2 oz (50 g) desiccated coconut

Preheat oven to 350°F (180°C, gas mark 4). Beat together butter, brown sugar, egg, water, black treacle and vanilla. Stir in remaining ingredients. Drop by teaspoonfuls on to greased baking sheet. Bake for 12 to 15 minutes. Remove from baking sheet immediately. Makes about 60 biscuits.

CHAPTER SEVEN

Sex during Pregnancy

Pregnancy can be a time of emotional strain in a relationship, partly because of the mood swings you may be feeling, and partly because you and your partner are trying to adjust to your impending new roles. Sex during pregnancy can vary between a physical closeness that brings you both together and an obligation which one of you ends up resenting. It can be a time of sexual tension, partially because some women aren't sure what is OK in pregnancy, and they are embarrassed to ask. A sensitive doctor or midwife should be able to address your questions without adding to your embarrassment. You also should bear in mind that a simple question such as "Will deep penetration hurt the baby?" can be answered in a few moments and may make you feel much more comfortable with sex during the months of your pregnancy. This in turn will alleviate some potential problems between you and your partner, so if you have a question, don't hesitate to ask it. This chapter addresses the concerns that most women (and men) have during pregnancy.

Is having sex going to hurt me or my baby?

Your baby is very well protected by the strong muscular uterus, the bag of waters and your pelvic bones. Sexual intercourse, masturbation or orgasm will not hurt your baby, just as most other activities won't hurt your baby. Occasionally very vigorous and deep penetration may cause you to bleed a little bit. This can be terrifying when it happens, but usually the blood comes from the cervix. This opening to your uterus is engorged with blood during pregnancy and tends to bleed very easily. Should this happen to you, don't panic. Put on a sanitary towel, lie down with your feet elevated a little bit, and try to relax. Note how much blood there is, and contact your doctor or midwife in the morning. Most of the time, you won't have more than a 2-inch (5 cm) spot on the sanitary towel.

If you are bleeding very heavily after intercourse (soaking a towel within an hour), you should probably contact your doctor or midwife right away for instructions. That amount of bleeding may indicate that the placenta is covering, or close to, the cervix and the jarring has caused an excessive amount of bleeding. If that is the case, a diagnosis is made with an ultrasound scan, and you may be instructed to avoid intercourse altogether until the uterus grows, thereby pulling the placenta away from the cervix. You will need another ultrasound scan to show you this. On very rare occasions, the placenta remains over the cervix (placenta praevia; *see* p. 172) and vaginal penetration is prohibited. Please note that these are rare instances, and *most* of the time, sexual intercourse is perfectly safe and pleasurable.

I don't seem to be interested in sex. Is that normal?

The most common times to be uninterested in sex during pregnancy is during the first trimester when all you want to do is sleep, and during the last two months, when you are physically uncomfortable and the movement of the baby can be most distracting. These are very normal feelings, and you should be very open and honest with your partner about it. The end of pregnancy is also a time when many women feel that they are unattractive and very unsexy.

Your lack of interest can become a problem if your partner's need and desire for sex are a great deal more than your need and desire. Remember, infrequent sex is not a problem if both parties are satisfied with the frequency. Conflicts only arise when one of you wants sex more often than the other. If you have a lack of interest in sex, and it is the source of growing conflict between the two of you, sort out your feelings. Is it because you don't feel attractive? If so, let your partner know that you need reassurance that he is still as attracted to you. If the movements of the baby are distracting you during sex, perhaps it will help to change positions so the movements aren't as intense. Also try not to eat anything sweet a few hours before sex, as sugar will make the baby more active.

Are there any activities I should avoid during sex?

Intercourse, as stated before, is usually fine during pregnancy. There are a couple of instances, though, when you will be instructed to avoid it. One of these times is after your "waters" have broken. The sac or membranes in which the baby lives inside the uterus protects you and the baby from infection. Once these membranes have broken, there is a pathway for bacteria to reach the baby and the lining of the uterus. The vagina is not a sterile environment, but the bacteria there usually do not move upward, but rather downward and out of the vaginal opening. The insertion of the penis (or anything else, such as fingers, vibrators, douches or tampons) will allow bacteria to reach the uterus and make you much more susceptible to an infection. Sexual intercourse is always taboo after your waters have broken.

Another time that sexual intercourse is not recommended is if you are having any vaginal bleeding at any time during your pregnancy. Early in the pregnancy, bleeding may be the sign of an impending miscarriage, and you should avoid sex until your doctor tells you that you are no longer at risk of a miscarriage. At other times during the pregnancy, bleeding may indicate placenta praevia (when the placenta covers all or part of the cervix), and intercourse may cause some serious bleeding (*see above* and p. 99). Again, wait until your doctor says it's OK to go ahead with intercourse. The placenta will often move away from your cervix as the pregnancy progresses.

Apart from any complications with the pregnancy, there are two activities which should be avoided even in the healthiest of pregnancies. One is anal intercourse, when there is a great chance of spreading some harmful bacteria to the vagina and, subsequently, the cervix. In addition, it is unlikely that a woman with haemorrhoids would find anal sex pleasurable.

The other activity involves oral sex. Generally, oral sex is fine during pregnancy. However, your partner should never, ever blow air into the vagina. This can cause a serious complication called *air embolus*, in which the air travels through the bloodstream to the lungs, which could possibly result in death.

It's really uncomfortable with my partner on top of me. What can I do?

During the first part of pregnancy, before your belly starts to get noticeably bigger, you may be quite comfortable with your partner on top of you. However, as your belly starts to grow and the baby moves more, that position becomes increasingly uncomfortable either for you or your partner or for both of you. Fortunately, there are many different positions you can try during sexual intercourse. Practise, and see which ones work for both of you.

One of the things you can do is to place lots of pillows under your buttocks. That will put you in a position that will keep the bulk of your partner's weight off your abdomen, as long as he supports his torso with his arms. You could also try lying on your side, with him behind you on his side. In fact, towards the end of pregnancy, most of the comfortable positions involve having him behind you, either with you on your side, or on all fours. Go easy when trying a new position. Most of the time, having the man at the back allows for deeper penetration, and that may be uncomfortable for you. You can also try sitting on top of your partner in a semi-squat. (That's also good exercise for your legs for labour!)

The important thing to remember is that good communication leads to a more satisfying and enjoyable sex life. This is especially true during pregnancy. You need to be honest with your partner about your desire for sex (or lack of it), and to be very vocal about what feels good and what doesn't. This can be a time when you are extremely active sexually (often because you don't have to worry about birth control), or it can be a time when you enjoy your time alone together in other ways. If you are feeling unsexy, it helps to talk about it, and to realize that you are not the only woman who feels this way. However, if you think about it, pregnancy is the most feminine thing in the world!

CHAPTER EIGHT

Hazards in Pregnancy

The goal of producing the healthiest possible baby is directly dependent upon maintaining the mother's good health. Sometimes this is in conflict with the baby's well-being, and a balance must be struck between the two. Two living beings, whose needs are not identical, are being dealt with at the same time. And yet, this unit of mother, baby and placenta cannot be separated. Almost everything to which the mother is exposed and which she ingests passes in some degree to the foetus. It is essential to create the healthiest possible maternal environment so that the baby can flourish.

Women of childbearing age must at all times consider what effects their environment, their nutrition and the chemicals they ingest and produce could potentially have on a forming embryo. Even if you are not planning to become pregnant, maintaining your best possible health is in your own best interests. Then, should you inadvertently become pregnant, you will not have to look back with fear, guilt or shame that you may have exposed your unborn baby to potential hazards. And it is in the first trimester, and particularly in the first eight weeks of pregnancy (while the foetal organs are forming), that the baby is most susceptible to severe damage.

Medical problems

If you have a medical condition, especially one that requires medication, and you are of childbearing age, discuss the effects of your medical situation with your doctor or the consultant treating you. Medical problems which could affect a foetus, and the drugs used to treat those problems, should be discussed *prior* to conception. Many women in this situation arrive at their doctor's surgery or at the antenatal clinic already pregnant, when the opportunity has passed for adjusting, discontinuing or trying different medical regimens which may be safer in pregnancy.

However, if you are taking medications, do not simply discontinue them if you are considering becoming pregnant or if you think you already are pregnant. Consult your family doctor or consultant, or those caring for you antenatally. If there is a national organization and/or support group for those with your medical condition, it can be useful to get in touch with them to find out the latest information on drug effects and the management of your condition during pregnancy.

Your own good health is paramount. If maintaining your health depends on taking medication, then the particular medication chosen must offer more potential benefit than potential harm to you and your baby. This balance can sometimes prove to be very tricky. There are some medical conditions where treatment is essential to the mother, and yet all of the treatment choices are seriously dangerous to foetal development and growth. It is critical for a woman who may face this unusual dilemma to consider all of her options, including not bearing children, prior to becoming pregnant.

Women with particular medical problems or who require medication in the long term need to be followed more closely by their midwife and doctor. It is also important to seek antenatal care early in the pregnancy. As the foetus grows inside you, it puts different demands on your body as the pregnancy progresses. So don't be surprised if the dose of your medication needs to be changed from time to time. Don't feel as if something is going wrong if the dose you usually require needs to be increased. Listen to your body and contact your doctor if you think that your medication level needs adjusting. By doing all you can to maintain your best possible health, you will be providing your baby with the best possible environment in which to grow. Continuously fretting over whether the baby is all right is not really in the baby's best interest. Chemicals are not only obtained from a chemist's shop. Your own body produces chemicals and hormones all the time; these are the substances which control and modify your bodily functions. If you are constantly obsessed with and worrying over every minute of your pregnancy, your anxiety hormones will pass to the foetus. These stress hormones are called *catecholamines*, and in very large doses they are considered detrimental to foetal well-being. This does not mean that your pregnancy is not designed to handle stress; if you are confronted by a seriously stressful situation (such as a family bereavement or the loss of a job), your baby will not be harmed by your normal emotions of grief or anxiety. It is the constant state of anxiety or stress which seems to be most detrimental to the foetus. Try to relax and accept your pregnancy. You cannot "control" your pregnancy, so try to adjust your life to meet its demands and needs. Avoid excesses in diet, exercise and emotional obsessions.

Possible hazards

There are, however, factors which you can and should be aware of and control to the best of your ability. These include medications, environmental pollutants, and addictive drugs such as alcohol, cigarettes and "recreational" drugs.

The degree to which the foetus is adversely affected by environmental substances and/or drugs is directly related to four factors: (1) the dose of the substance or drug; (2) the timing of the exposure to the substance or drug; (3) the duration of exposure; and (4) exposure to two or more substances or drugs simultaneously, allowing the two factors to interact and cause potentially harmful effects. With all these variables, it is easy to see that if the foetus is adversely affected during a pregnancy, it is usually very difficult to pinpoint the offending agent.

The range of effects on the foetus may be so subtle as to be insignificant or may be so severe as to cause foetal death. There are very few drugs known to be definitely fatal to foetus (abortifacient) or definitely known to cause foetal malformations (teratogenic). Two drugs known to cause congenital abnormalities – diethylstilboesterol (DES) and Thalidomide – have been taken off the market. Other drugs are strongly suspected of causing foetal defects. There are also rare drugs or environmental agents which can even sow the seeds for cancer (carcinogens) or genetic mutations (mutagens) later in the life of the foetus. Most drugs do not fall in any of these categories but have an unknown potential for damage. During the first three weeks after conception, a very hazardous agent in a sufficiently high dose is most likely to cause miscarriage. From the third to the tenth week, as the embryo's limbs and organs are forming, a very hazardous agent is most likely to cause either a malformation or a functional defect. Exposure to hazardous agents in the second and third trimesters generally causes less obvious defects but may affect foetal growth.

The following is a list of agents to which many pregnant women may be exposed. It is designed to give you some basic information on the agent and indicate when exposure warrants medical consultation.

Alcohol   There is no question that excessive consumption of alcohol can cause a number of malformations – growth retardation both before and after birth, mental retardation, jitteriness and developmental delays, as well as abnormalities in the look of the face – which together are called the *foetal alcohol syndrome*. Other problems seen in this syndrome include limb defects, problems in the development of the bladder and genital system, and heart defects.

The mothers of babies who are born with these abnormalities generally had four to five drinks per day. It is important to remember that alcohol is a drug, and its effects are dose-related; if less alcohol is consumed, there may be more subtle symptoms in the foetus. Alcohol intake very early in the pregnancy (the first 3–5 weeks) has been associated with an increased rate of miscarriage and decreased developmental and intellectual growth in those babies that are not miscarried.

Since the degree of damage to a baby is definitely related to how much alcohol is drunk, what is a safe amount of alcohol during pregnancy? Because alcohol definitely crosses the placenta, THERE IS NO SAFE AMOUNT OF ALCOHOL DURING PREGNANCY.

Does this mean that you can never drink any alcohol during pregnancy? Avoiding alcohol entirely is often advised and is not a bad idea. However, you must keep in mind that alcohol is one of the oldest drugs of civilization, and that many of our foremothers probably drank some alcohol during pregnancy. While there is no "safe" amount of any drug in pregnancy, for many women alcohol is a good relaxant when taken very occasionally and in great moderation. It is clear that chronic alcohol consumption and binge drinking will be bad for you and your foetus. But if you create a flood of anxiety hormones instead of drinking a very small and infrequent amount of alcohol, this is not in the baby's interests either. The point is not to brood over the occasional glass of wine with dinner, the celebratory glass of champagne, the cold lager on a summer's night or the small

There are a number of potential hazards that every pregnant woman should try to avoid — among them, industrial chemicals, pre-packed foods such as salads (which may contain the listeria bacteria), non-prescribed and illicit drugs, alcoholic drinks and cigarettes.

glass of sherry on a cold evening. Just enjoy these rare treats and keep them to a minimum.

Antacids Most over-the-counter antacid preparations are considered safe during pregnancy. Antacids generally contain either aluminium hydroxide, calcium carbonate or magnesium compounds. The aluminium and calcium products may cause constipation, whereas the magnesium compounds may cause loose stools. The use of sodium bicarbonate is not recommended during pregnancy as its short duration of action can cause a sharp and rapid return of symptoms. In addition, it is readily absorbed into the bloodstream, where it can cause a change in the normal acid/alkaline balance in both the mother and the baby.

Antibiotics In the event of a severe bacterial infection, an antibiotic is called for and there are many which have not been shown to harm the foetus in any way. More than 99 per cent of colds are caused by viruses and are not helped by the use of antibiotics. Non-viral pneumonias, on the other hand, respond beautifully to antibiotics and these should be prescribed in such cases. In other words, if you need an antibiotic, by all means take it. Don't drag on with a curable infectious disease because you are afraid to take medication during your pregnancy. Remember your good health ensures the best environment for your baby. If you are prescribed an antibiotic and you have any doubts as to its safety in pregnancy, discuss this with the person who prescribed it.

Common antibiotics which are considered "safe" in pregnancy and are frequently prescribed include the penicillins (penicillin, ampicillin, amoxycillin, cloxacillin, etc.), erythromycin and the cephalosporins (Keflex, Velosef, Cefizox, Ceporex, etc.).

Sulphonamides (e.g. Gantrisin) and nitrofurantoin (Furadantin, Macrodantin) may be taken during the first two trimesters of pregnancy, when they can be very useful in the treatment of urinary tract infections, especially those which are resistant to ampicillin. They should not be used in the last trimester of pregnancy because of complications which may develop in the newborn if these drugs are taken at a time close to delivery.

Tuberculosis is often treated with a combination of two or more drugs. Isoniazid and ethambutol are the drugs of first choice; if a third drug is required, rifampicin is usually the drug chosen, even though its safety in pregnancy is debatable. A mother with active TB is a sick mother and should be treated. As in all antenatal problems, she should discuss and understand the risks of her disease and her medications so that she may participate in the decision-making process of her treatment.

There are antibiotics whose use in pregnancy is controversial and which should not be chosen in the initial treatment of an infection if they can be avoided. Metronidazole (Flagyl) falls into this category. Although almost all research indicates that this drug does not cause birth defects, there is a study which suggests that it may cause cancer in rats. However, the evidence against metronidazole is not sufficiently strong to preclude its use in pregnancy when it is absolutely necessary.

The tetracyclines (including doxycycline) *should not* be used during pregnancy. They cross the placenta and, in early pregnancy, they can cause impaired bone growth in the foetus, and in later pregnancy they can cause permanent staining of the teeth and deformities in bone growth.

Anti-convulsants Disorders in which convulsions (epileptic seizures, "fits") play a part can be caused by many different factors and, as a result, many different treatments are recommended. Because most seizure disorders begin before the age of 20, many women of child-bearing age are already on medications. It is crucial that you discuss your medications with your doctor or consultant neurologist prior to becoming pregnant. Most anti-convulsant medications do cross the placenta, and many affect the foetus adversely, some severely. So it is important to evaluate the status of your condition and change your drugs to those which cause the least harm to the foetus, while still controlling your seizures. Sometimes this re-evaluation even allows some women to discontinue anti-convulsant therapy entirely. Babies born to epileptic women taking anti-convulsant medications have two to three times the incidence of birth defects when compared with the general population; thus about 10 per cent of babies born to these women are affected. However, it is very hard to separate the effects of the condition from the effects of the treatment.

Certain anti-convulsants have been more implicated in causing birth defects than others. Phenytoin (Epanutin) has been associated with a birth defect rate of over 15 per cent in humans. The "foetal hydantoin syndrome" includes growth retardation in the womb and after birth, mental retardation, small head size, prominent facial features (including low-set ears, broad bridge of the nose, possible cleft lip and/or palate, short nose, wide mouth, small chin and other anomalies), and poorly developed fingers, toes and nails. If you are taking phenytoin or any other anti-convulsant and find out you are pregnant, do not stop the drug; instead, consult with your doctor at once. Modifications in your drug regimen may still be able to be made without risking sudden discontinuation of your drugs and reactivation of your epileptic condition.

Anti-depressants There is insufficient information about any ill-effects on the foetus from mothers taking anti-depressant medications. This is particularly true of the family of anti-depressants called tricyclic anti-depressants (Elavil, Sinequan, Tofranil), which are not recommended in pregnancy if their use can be avoided. Again, if you are on long-term anti-depressant therapy, discuss your condition and treatment with your doctor *prior* to becoming pregnant.

Lithium, used in the treatment of manic-depressive illness, has been associated with certain heart defects in babies, especially if the level of it in the mother's blood is allowed to become intermittently high. Therefore, it is important to take this drug in small frequent doses, to prevent fluctuating levels. Other birth defects have been loosely associated with this medication. As with all drugs which may affect the foetus, this drug is not prescribed in pregnancy unless it is truly necessary.

Aspirin This is one of the oldest and most commonly taken medications available. Its use during pregnancy is widespread – in fact, so widespread that it is difficult to determine what effects aspirin actually has on the foetus because there are so few women who have not taken some aspirin, even inadvertently, during the nine months of their pregnancy. Large amounts taken during pregnancy, either intermittent high doses or long-term use, have been shown to have harmful effects on both the mother and the foetus, the most harmful when aspirin has been taken in the final weeks of pregnancy. The effects on the mother include delay in the onset of labour, prolonged labour, and increased bleeding before, during or after delivery. The effects on the baby include an increased tendency to bleed, skin rash, increased intracranial (inside the skull) bleeding (particularly in premature infants) and possible growth retardation.

Currently, experts recommend that aspirin should *not* be used as a mild pain killer or to reduce fever during pregnancy; for these common problems, paracetamol is preferred. It must be noted, however, that daily low doses of aspirin have recently been recommended for the treatment of certain medical conditions (e.g. lupus) during pregnancy. So if you have taken the occasional aspirin during your pregnancy, don't become obsessed by the possible harm you may have caused your baby. Your aim should be to keep your aspirin consumption to a minimum during your pregnancy if medically possible. If you have a medical condition for which aspirin is required, you should be carefully monitored by your doctor.

Aspartame (brand name = NutraSweet) This latest in sugar substitutes has been extensively studied and has not yet been proven harmful to the foetus, although some isolated reports have questioned aspartame's safety in pregnancy. However, natural sweeteners such as sugar and honey are truly safe in pregnancy. Since overindulging in sweets is not recommended at any time, why not use the safest natural sweeteners in moderation and thereby avoid any of the possible (although as yet undetermined) effects of aspartame or any other sugar substitutes.

Asthma medications Asthma is a very common medical problem, and the control of its symptoms during pregnancy is essential. As with other long-standing medical conditions, you should discuss the drugs that you are taking with your doctor *before* you become pregnant. Since asthma may get better or worse or stay the same during your pregnancy, it may become necessary to change your medications or their dosages at some time.

The most common medication used to control asthma is theophylline (and the related drug aminophylline), and it has not been shown to have any ill effects on the foetus. It is important to monitor the mother's blood level of theophylline because severely elevated levels of the drug can cause side-effects in her such as jitteriness and nausea. If a baby is born to a mother with toxic levels of theophylline, it may be irritable and nauseous and may vomit.

Sodium cromoglycate (Intal) is very useful in preventing asthma attacks when taken prior to exposure to a known allergen (such as animals or exercise). It is not recommended for the treatment of an asthma attack; its use should be only as a preventive medication, and in this role it is very effective. It has not been found to have any adverse effects on the foetus.

If the asthma cannot be controlled with sodium cromoglycate and/ or theophylline, orciprenaline (Alupent) may be either inhaled or taken as a syrup or injection. It can be used with the above two medications during pregnancy. There are no studies showing harmful effects on the human foetus, although it can cause rapid pulse, palpitations, jitteriness, nausea and vomiting in the mother. Taking this drug may complicate the treatment of concurrent medical problems such as diabetes or high blood pressure.

Many asthma sufferers also have to take steroid drugs every now and again or in the long term. When inhaled, steroids seem to have no physical effect on the mother, other than to make it easier for her to breathe. The effects on the foetus are not known but studies done thus far have not shown an increase in birth defects. If the woman has a severe asthma attack, she may need to take steroids by mouth or, in emergency situations, intravenously. Although there is evidence that steroid therapy during the first trimester of pregnancy is associated with a small increase in birth defects (particularly cleft lip and palate), if you require steroid drugs to control your asthma, take the medications you need. Do not allow your asthma to get out of control in an effort to avoid taking them. On the other hand, if you have a number of medications from which to choose, do not randomly select one from your pre-pregnancy supply without first consulting your doctor.

Caffeine   Caffeine and the related compound theophylline are found in coffee, tea, chocolate and many soft drinks. Women have been taking the first three for many centuries and the last for over 100 years. If taken in moderation, they have not been shown to have any harmful effects on the foetus. Caffeine does cross the placenta and can stimulate the baby and cause an increase in its activity. This increased activity is not bad for the baby; however, drinking 8–25 cups of coffee per day can cause irritability of the foetal central nervous system and jitteriness in the newborn. As with many other pregnancy-related activities, when it comes to caffeine intake moderation is the key. If you are used to consuming five or six cups of coffee or tea a day, cut back to one or two cups at most.

Cannabis (Marijuana)   There is a large body of evidence which shows the harmful effects of cannabis on the foetus. It readily crosses the placenta and passes to the baby, where it may depress its heart rate and cause changes in its brain waves. Cannabis also has many of the same dangerous effects seen in tobacco smoking. In both cases, the toxin-laden smoke is inhaled into lungs, but in most instances, cannabis smoke is inhaled more deeply and held in the lungs for as long as the smoker is able. Cannabis use is associated with decreased function of the placenta, which can lead to an increase in miscarriage, premature delivery and stillbirth. Long-term cannabis use can lead to a low birth weight infant and has been linked to foetal anomalies similar to those found in alcohol-exposed babies (*see* Alcohol *above*). Newborns who have been exposed to cannabis in the womb tend to be more irritable and have more problems feeding and sleeping.

Cats   Cats' faeces can carry the parasite that causes toxoplasmosis (*see* p. 165).

Cheeses (soft)   These can contain listeria bacteria (*see* p. 164).

Cocaine   This is absolutely harmful to you and to your baby. In fact, cocaine is even more harmful to the foetus because it crosses the placenta and lingers in the foetal environment for many days, continuously exposing the baby to its harmful effects until the drug is finally excreted. If taken in the first trimester, cocaine greatly increases the risk of miscarriage. If taken later in pregnancy, it affects the baby's developing central nervous system and can cause lasting developmental damage. It can also damage the placenta, thereby interfering with the growth of the foetus (intra-uterine growth retardation) as well as placing the placenta at risk of rupturing from the uterus (*abruptio placenta*; *see* p. 172). Cocaine is clearly one of the most serious poisons to which you could expose your unborn baby.

Cold remedies Since most respiratory infections are caused by viruses (and therefore are cure-less), most cold remedies are designed only to alleviate some of their annoying symptoms. Nothing replaces good nutrition and lots of rest in the treatment of a cold. For a cough, inhaling steam for five minutes at least every four hours is very effective. In addition, drinking a cup of hot water, lemon and honey (with an optional cinnamon stick) helps clear the chest of congestion. For the treatment of a stuffy nose, placing hot compresses across your sinuses, from 1 inch (2.5 cm) above your brow to 1 inch (2.5 cm) below your cheekbones, helps drain the sinuses of mucus. For the treatment of a sore throat, gargling with salt water ($\frac{1}{2}$ teaspoon salt in 8 fl oz [230 ml] warm water) is very effective. Paracetamol is usually adequate treatment for the aches and pains of a common cold. Most cold remedies are not any more effective than these measures. In fact, if there were any one remedy which could truly make you feel better, there would be no need for the shelves full of preparations available for the treatment of the common cold.

If your cold symptoms do not respond to the above suggestions and you feel you would benefit from an antihistamine, a decongestant or cough medication, there are several choices of medications you could take which are not considered harmful in pregnancy. For a runny or stuffed nose, low-dose chlorpheniramine (Expulin), diphenhydramine (Benadryl), or pseudoephedrine (Sudafed) may be taken during pregnancy. The first two can cause drowsiness, whereas the latter can cause palpitations. For the treatment of a cough, dextromethorphan (Cosylan) is a good cough suppressant and is contained in many cough syrups (e.g. Lotussin). If the cough is so severe that the usual cough remedies do not work, contact your doctor. Sometimes codeine may be necessary; this drug has been in use for many years, and in the small quantities necessary for cough

113

suppression it is not considered harmful to the foetus. It may, however, cause you to become drowsy and constipated.

Diarrhoea medications   Most bouts of diarrhoea caused by intestinal viruses are miserable but short lived. The key to their treatment is the replacement of fluid and salts. This can be adequately accomplished with Lucozade or chicken broth. A diet of broth, dry ginger, cola, rice, cream crackers, apple juice or apple sauce will usually keep you stable until your immune system can get rid of the virus or other infective agent. If these remedies are not effective, you may use Kaolin (Kaopectate) after you have consulted your doctor; however, avoid Kaolin and Morphine. Your doctor will surely want to investigate more serious causes of severe and unremitting loose stools.

Diuretics   Swelling during pregnancy is a common problem but should not be treated with diuretics, drugs that cause the body to lose excess fluid. Resting on your side with your legs raised, wearing support tights and getting off your feet are far more effective in reducing the feet and ankle swelling of pregnancy. Diuretics pull fluid from your circulation and can potentially reduce blood flow to the placenta. For this reason, diuretics are controversial even in the treatment of high blood pressure during pregnancy. If you have had long-standing high blood pressure which is well controlled on diuretics, consult with your doctor prior to becoming pregnant. It may be advisable to change your blood pressure medications; however, in some cases, well-tolerated diuretic therapy is not discontinued. It is thought that, in these long-standing cases, diuretics may not, in fact, be harmful in pregnancy.

Food additives   Many of the foods we eat today have been exposed to chemicals, some beneficial and some harmful. You should not become obsessed about every ingredient you eat or drink, but you must be cautious and try to avoid harmful chemical additives. Cooking from scratch allows you to control which ingredients go into your food. The results are tastier, less expensive and more nutritious than most prepared foods. If you do eat prepared foods, try to avoid (whether pregnant or not) food containing chemical dyes and preservatives. These include nitrates and nitrites (found in luncheon-type meats), sulphites (used to keep seafood and cut vegetables looking fresh), and monosodium glutamate (MSG). Wash and/or

114

peel all fresh fruits in an effort to avoid insecticides. The effects that these chemicals may have on the foetus are not known, but since they are not recommended for general human consumption, they are best avoided in pregnancy.

Heroin/methadone Both of these easily cross the placenta and pass to the foetus, which then becomes addicted to either drug. Drug withdrawal in the mother causes drug withdrawal in the foetus, and this is associated with an increased rate of stillbirth; for this reason, neither drug should be suddenly discontinued in pregnancy. Nevertheless both drugs are very harmful to the unborn baby. Both can cause poor growth leading to a higher rate of foetal distress in labour as well as poor mental and physical development for many years after birth. When heroin- and methadone-addicted newborns go through drug withdrawal, symptoms can include jitteriness, seizures, poor feeding and poor sleep patterns.

Heroin addicts, in addition, usually have multiple other medical problems. Poor nutrition is common as is addiction to other drugs and to alcohol. They have many problems with infection – HIV and AIDS, hepatitis type B, infected skin sites, and blood-borne infections which can damage the heart.

Hormones Some women inadvertently take hormone-containing preparations, such as birth control pills or hormones designed to bring on a period, prior to learning that they are pregnant. Each individual preparation may have a somewhat different effect on the foetus.

DES (diethylstilboestrol) is an oestrogen-containing compound, and its use in the 1950s and 1960s to prevent miscarriage was found in later years to create major problems in the affected offspring. In the male children, abnormal sperm formation has been found when these boys become adults. In the female children, many complications have appeared, ranging from the rare but dreadful development of vaginal cancer at the time of puberty to abnormalities of the cervix and uterus causing problems of infertility. However, certain hormone preparations, such as natural progesterone, are sometimes recommended in early pregnancy to prevent miscarriage, and have thus far been shown to cause no harmful effects in the foetus.

The most common hormone-containing preparations taken early in pregnancy are birth control pills. Again, the exact formulation and hormone content of the pill is important. In general, these preparations have not been shown to cause the heart defects that were once ascribed to them. This is also true for medroxyprogesterone (e.g. Provera), a drug commonly used to bring on a period in women who have menstrual irregularities. Both groups of medications have been shown to have some effect on foetal genitals, the range of effects depending on the hormone content, the dose and the time period during which it was taken, as well as the sex of the foetus. However, the percentage of affected foetuses is very small when compared to the number of women who inadvertently take hormones while pregnant.

Industrial chemicals and insecticides   Many of these are harmful both to you and your baby. If you are planning to become pregnant and your work requires that you are in contact with strong chemicals, contact your union (if you belong to one), the Health & Safety Executive and/or your local authority Environmental Health Officers, and consult with them regarding the safety of the specific chemicals. The London Hazards Centre (3rd floor, Headland House, 308 Gray's Inn Road, London WC1X 8DS, tel: 01-837 5605) also has information on thousands of different hazards. If you find that the chemicals you are working with are indeed potentially harmful, ask your employer if you can change your job prior to and during your pregnancy. Even if the chemicals with which you work are considered "safe", it is important that you try to avoid inhaling any chemical fumes or absorbing any chemicals through your skin. Always work in a well-ventilated space and wear a protective mask and non-porous gloves. If your employer refuses to remove you from work that is potentially damaging to your baby, you can leave and take the company to an industrial tribunal to get compensation.

Laxatives   Constipation is a very common problem in pregnancy and its treatment should be based on good long-term nutritional habits. Adequate fibre and water intake are the keys to regular bowel function. However, if this is insufficient in preventing constipation, then a bulk-forming laxative (Metamucil) may be taken as long as water intake is further increased. Stool softeners (e.g. Dioctyl, Dorbanex) may also be used safely in pregnancy. Both of these additional measures take some time to work and may not produce the instant relief which you are seeking. You should try to maintain good bowel function over the long term so as not to require a harsher remedy.

If you do become so severely constipated that you need the occasional strong laxative, natural ones such as senna (found in senna tea and in products such as Senokot) or cascara are preferable to harsher laxatives containing magnesium, sodium or potassium salts. These latter products can cause a more intense fluid loss and result in dehydration. Products containing aloe are best avoided as they cross the placenta and cause an increase in the bowel movements of the foetus and allow foetal faeces (*meconium*) to pass while the baby is still in the womb. Castor oil should also be avoided as it can stimulate labour in late pregnancy.

Meat (undercooked, raw)   This can contain the parasite that causes toxoplasmosis (*see* p. 165).

Paint   If you are planning to decorate or renovate before the baby's arrival, choose low-risk products such as water-based emulsion paint and make sure you work in a well-ventilated room. Better yet, try to get someone else to do the painting, return home only after it has dried for a few hours so that you minimize your exposure to any fumes. Paint strippers and paint thinners tend to release carbon monoxide and should not be used by pregnant women. A pre-World War II flat or house will most likely contain lead-based paint, which is especially toxic to pregnant women. In addition, it is best to avoid the use of oil-based paints.

Paracetamol   This mild pain killer and fever medication has not been shown to cause any harmful effects to the foetus when taken as prescribed. The drug does cross the placenta but has not been shown to produce any foetal defects. *Excessive* use of the drug in or out of pregnancy is not recommended as it may cause liver damage in the mother. Two tablets every four hours as needed is the recommended dosage. If this dosage is not adequate in the control of pain or fever, your doctor or midwife should be consulted.

Perms and hair colourings   Permanent waves and hair colouring products all contain chemicals which can be absorbed through the scalp and skin. Although there is no definitive data showing that they adversely affect the foetus, they should be used cautiously, if at all. Since your pregnancy can go along quite well without the use of these products, you may want to avoid using them until after your baby is born. If you find that your self-image really needs a boost and that a perm or a colour rinse would make you feel that much better, then carefully choose a product which is least absorbed into the hair and scalp. This means trying to avoid all permanent and semi-permanent dyes which contain coal tars, aromatic amines and diamines. Many hair-colouring products do not list their ingredients except in terms such as "No. 19 chestnut", and since their actual contents cannot be determined, these products should be avoided.

Pre-packed foods   Pre-packed salads and other foods kept in the cool refrigerators at supermarkets have been found to contain listeria bacteria (*see* p. 164).

Roaccutane (isotretinoin)   This prescription medication (available only from hospitals) is extremely effective in the treatment of cystic acne; however, it is known to cause severe birth defects if taken during pregnancy, particularly during the first trimester. These defects include abnormalities in the brain, ears, face and thymus, and in neurological development leading to mental retardation. If you have severe acne and are seeking treatment, talk to your consultant about the appropriateness of Roaccutane in the treatment of your condition. Include in that discussion your contraception and childbirth plans. Pregnancy *must* be avoided while taking this drug and for one month after stopping it.

Skin creams and ointments   Drugs can be easily absorbed through the skin. Therefore, skin preparations should be used judiciously in pregnancy. Creams containing steroids are used extensively for a variety of skin conditions, including eczema, psoriasis, nettle rash, burns, etc. Consult with your doctor regarding their use, but by all means do not let a skin condition get out of hand because you are pregnant and are afraid to use the appropriate skin treatment. Antibiotic ointments are available over-the-counter, are extremely useful in the treatment of skin infections and are generally regarded as safe in pregnancy.

Smoking   Cigarette smoking is without a doubt harmful to you and your baby. The nicotine, carbon monoxide and other toxins inhaled in cigarette smoke cross the placenta, where their concentration in the foetal environment is actually higher than in the mother's circulation. The more cigarettes a woman smokes during her pregnancy, the greater the detrimental effect that smoking will have on her baby. Cigarette smoking causes multiple complications of pregnancy, including: impaired placental function and small placenta size; increased rate of miscarriage; premature delivery; stillbirth; low birth weight infants; and the increased risk of premature separation of the placenta (*abruptio placenta*; *see* p. 172). Newborns of smokers are more prone to sudden infant death syndrome (SIDS), or "cot death".

Passive smoke – that is, smoked inhaled from the cigarettes of nearby smokers – is absorbed by you (and, of course, by your baby), though to a lesser degree than if you yourself smoke. Children who grow up in the homes of smokers are more prone to respiratory ailments. It is obvious that if you and/or someone in your household smokes, you should all try to quit prior to your becoming pregnant. You should discuss with your employer about getting moved away from smokers in the work place.

Nicotine chewing gum is not deemed "safe" in pregnancy; however, for some people, it provides the necessary crutch to help them quit the smoking habit. With the obviously bad effects caused by smoking on your unborn child, it is hard to imagine that nicotine chewing gum is more harmful than cigarette smoking. For this reason, if you believe that a short course of nicotine gum may enable you to quit smoking, use it even during pregnancy to carry you across the bridge from smoker to non-smoker.

Video display units (VDUs) and microwaves We are all exposed daily to the non-ionizing radiation of our modern world. Sources include microwave ovens, video display units, colour TVs, high-voltage power lines, TV and radio transmitters and CB radios. The effect of non-ionizing radiation (as opposed to the ionizing radiation of X-rays, *see below*) on the foetus is not known. As with other unknown but potentially hazardous environmental pollutants, try to limit your exposure during pregnancy. If you use your microwave oven frequently, stand back from it while it is in use. If your work requires you to be in constant close contact with a VDU, see if you can possibly arrange to perform other work-related duties. If you have any questions regarding the amount of exposure to non-ionizing radiation you receive at your work place, consult the agencies suggested under "Industrial chemicals and insecticides".

119

X-rays X-rays used to diagnose diseases and other medical and dental conditions should be avoided during pregnancy unless absolutely necessary. If you suspect that you may be pregnant, do not undergo any but the most urgent X-rays, and if they are not of the pelvis or lower abdomen, request a lead shield be placed over your pelvis. High doses of X-ray exposure are harmful to the foetus. In the first two weeks of pregnancy, excessive ionizing radiation increases the risk of miscarriage; from the 3rd to the 12th week, excessive X-rays can have deleterious effects on the forming nervous system. However, if an X-ray is absolutely essential in diagnosing a medical problem in pregnancy, it should be performed. Remember that your good health is the most important factor in the baby's well-being and if you are so seriously ill as to require an X-ray or surgery, then whatever needs to be done to restore your good health should be judiciously carried out.

CHAPTER NINE

Myths, Legends and Fallacies

There can be no more fertile ground for myths, legends, fallacies and fantasies than pregnancy. Family members, friends and even total strangers are always willing to give advice and provide you with pregnancy folklore. Try to keep it in perspective and accept it as a game or as part of an oral heritage. Do not let old wives' tales upset you; much of what is contained in them is misinformation. If you are bothered by a particular piece of "wisdom", read a more accurate source or ask your doctor or midwife about it. The following are some of the more common myths.

Baths Taking a hot bath during pregnancy is not only OK, but it is therapeutic. Whirlpools and jacuzzis are also relaxing and therapeutic. The water should not, however, be so hot as to make your skin bright red, nor should it make you feel lightheaded or dizzy. Hot-tubs are usually too hot and should be avoided.

Breasts The size of the breast has no correlation with the amount of milk it is capable of producing. Very small-breasted women can breastfeed just as well as large-breasted women.

Determining the sex There are a myriad of signs that supposedly "determine" the sex of the baby, and according to some, there are various rituals that can be performed to make sure you get a child of the sex you want. While many of these can be fun and are harmless, remember that every woman has a 50/50 chance of having either a boy or a girl. No ritual can predict the sex of a baby and only the genetic material contained in the fertilizing sperm can determine its sex.

Dental work   Good oral hygiene is part of your good health. You should have regular dental check-ups, and if you need dental work, you can and should have it done. Try to avoid having nitrous oxide and local anaesthetics containing adrenalin, and have only those X-rays which are necessary.

Food preference   Your eating habits during pregnancy will have no bearing on your child's likes or dislikes in food. Your favourite food will also not appear on your child as a birthmark.

Heartburn   Heartburn will not result in a hairy baby. Heartburn is common to most pregnancies, whereas hair distribution is usually determined by inheritance.

Inducing labour   Nothing will bring on labour until the cervix is ripe and the uterus is ready. Therefore, rides along a bumpy road, long hikes, Chinese food, raising your arms above your head and scrubbing the floor will not bring on labour. If they do, it is just coincidental. However, if you are ready to go into labour, orgasm and nipple stimulation can induce mild contractions and may just give the uterus the stimulus to induce labour. Likewise, taking a tablespoon of castor oil in a glass of orange juice for constipation will stimulate the release of substances called prostaglandins from the bowel which may precipitate the onset of labour. Taking more than one tablespoon can cause severe abdominal cramps and uncontrollable diarrhoea and will not enhance the desired result.

Seatbelts   Wearing your seatbelt will *not* harm the baby; in fact, it can potentially save the lives of both you and your baby if you are involved in a car accident.

Stretching and bending   Raising your arms above your head, bending at the waist or any other exercise will not cause the umbilical cord to wrap around the baby's neck, nor will the baby become strangled by its cord. These movements will also not induce labour.

Surgery   If you require emergency surgery at any time during your pregnancy, it is in your and your baby's best interests to have it done. Discuss with your doctor or the consultant caring for you which is the best choice of anaesthesia for your particular case; if you require general anaesthesia, then have it. Elective surgery is best put off until after the baby is born.

Travel   A ride in the pressurized cabin of an aircraft will not bring on labour. Air travel is as safe during pregnancy as it is at any other time. Try to take an occasional walk up and down the aisle so that your feet and ankles do not swell excessively. Near the end of pregnancy, you probably won't want to be far from home, and, in any event, many airlines refuse to carry women in the later stages of pregnancy.

Working   It is up to you when you stop working. Some health conditions may require that you curtail or stop work early in your pregnancy. But if your pregnancy has been uneventful, you may continue working as long as you are comfortable doing so. There is no right or wrong time to stop.

CHAPTER TEN

The Father and Other Supporters

The childbirth experience of fathers has come a long way since the days when Dad used to pace in a waiting room with other fathers smoking cigars. Men are now more involved with their partners' experiences throughout the pregnancy, and it is now more the norm for the father to be present at the actual birth.

The father's role in pregnancy

As men have become more involved, more research has been done exploring the father's feelings and concerns about his impending fatherhood. Men are also more involved now in rearing and "hands on" care of their infants and children. Some speculate that they feel more bonded to their children since they share the birth experience and, therefore, more a part of their children's lives.

Society has also changed. More and more women are in the workplace, and therefore demand that their partners take a more active role in household and childcare activities. As a result, men are slowly shedding their stereotype of "ruling the roost", and are becoming more accustomed to sharing their feelings and participating in activities that were formerly women's alone. Pregnancy and childbirth are surely two of those areas.

Like the woman, many of the initial feelings that a man has about becoming a father have to do with whether the pregnancy was planned or not. If it was and the baby is greatly wanted, excitement and anticipation usually abound when the pregnancy is confirmed. Following close behind, however, is some amount of anxiety and a fear of the unknown. If he is becoming a father for the first time, those feelings are usually somewhat more exaggerated. Many questions may surface about his competency as a father, how the pregnancy will change his relationship with his partner, how he will provide for his growing family financially, especially if his partner has been contributing substantially to the family income. This is also a time when many (resolved or unresolved) childhood memories become strangely significant. Men start to wonder if they will be as good a father as their own fathers were. Or will they be better? Will it be easier for them because they may be more financially secure than their fathers were, or will it be much more difficult because life seems so complex now? This is a period of intense soul searching for men as well as women. It helps so much if you can both talk about it together and share your concerns, fears and joys.

If the pregnancy was not a planned one, then the man has a lot of adjusting to do, just as his partner has. Feelings of anger, frustration, resentment and depression are not uncommon, nor are they unrealistic when faced with the news of such a life-altering event. Men do not have to deal with hormonal changes and nausea on top of the emotional strain, but it can be a difficult time for them just the same. It is helpful for both of you, when faced with an unplanned pregnancy, to set out priorities and discuss your innermost feelings when deciding what steps to take. As always, an open compassionate relationship makes coping much easier. If one or both of you are unable to resolve a conflict involving an unwanted pregnancy, professional counselling is probably the best advice.

Dealing with your feelings

The first feeling that most impending fathers experience about a pregnancy, especially if it is a planned one, is the joy and excitement that can be gained from telling others and boasting about the fact. It never ceases to amaze most fathers, when they reflect on what is happening inside their partners' bodies, that they have helped to create another human being who is growing right before their eyes. This is just one of many emotional thrills a father feels during the pregnancy and birth experience. These special feelings are felt as every major milestone is reached: the exhilaration of hearing the baby's heartbeat, the amazement of feeling it kick and move, the awe of seeing its ultrasound image, the excitement of seeing the head crowning moments before the birth and the tremendous high felt when witnessing the birth and holding your child for the first time. For most men, the births of their children, and especially their first one, are the most memorable moments in their lives. It truly is an experience hard to recapture in words.

Along with the excitement during the pregnancy, the father feels the promise and apprehension that anticipation of the birth brings as well as the anxiety of the event and what is to come after. While he will never know the physical and psychological feelings that the woman is experiencing during the long nine months, the man will undergo his own emotional changes that, in part, have a lot to do with the many unknowns related to pregnancy and birth.

One of the most constructive ways of dealing with the feelings of anxiety is to become involved as much as possible in the pregnancy. This includes going to the antenatal appointments with your partner and asking questions of those caring for her. Keep a list of questions and concerns that come up so that you won't forget to ask at the appropriate time. Become well informed. Read a lot about what is happening within your partner's body. Understanding the physical process will alleviate a great deal of anxiety, and give you a better idea of what to expect and how to be prepared for it. Throughout the pregnancy, talk to friends who have gone through the same thing. Sharing these (often funny) stories about coping with a pregnant woman's discomforts and mood swings will give you a sense of comradeship and will make you feel that you are not alone. However, keep in mind that no two pregnancies are alike – what may suit a friend and his partner may not suit you and yours.

At the end of the second trimester of the pregnancy, you will have the opportunity to accompany your partner to childbirth classes if she chooses to go. By all means, make every effort to attend these classes with her as they offer a social setting to share experiences with other couples, as well as giving you much valuable information about preparing for and participating in childbirth. These are constructive actions which will enhance the experience for both of you.

Talking about your concerns with your partner is probably one of the healthiest things a man can do for a relationship. Men often find it difficult to express their feelings and, as a result, act in different ways when something is troubling them. One of the extremes is for men to stay out later than they usually do, drink more heavily and/or downright ignore their partners during the pregnancy. When asked for an explanation by their perplexed and unhappy partners, they may withdraw even further.

This behaviour may be an outward sign of the man's inner turmoil about his impending fatherhood. He may feel that a noose is tightening around his neck. The thought of the reduction in freedom that a baby imposes can be quite frightening, and some men try to run away from it. This makes it extremely difficult for their pregnant partners who are trying to deal with their emotions and can't understand this change in their partners' personality.

If one or both of you see this pattern emerging in the early part of the pregnancy, it is best to have an airing of pent-up emotions, even if it involves a full-blown argument. Discuss the physical and emotional needs you both have, and see if you can reach an agreement or compromise on what behaviour will be acceptable to both of you.

The other extreme is the man who dotes on his pregnant partner. Some men may be so concerned (mostly from being misled or ill-informed) that their partners will hurt themselves or their babies by doing even the least strenuous of everyday activities, that the men drive the women crazy with attention. This usually appears to be sweet devotion at the beginning, but may all too soon turn into oppressive (and obsessive) nagging. Again, communication and accurate information will alleviate the tension which accumulates with this situation.

Changes in the relationship during pregnancy

There will be many changes in the relationship between the father and his partner during the pregnancy. For the most part, these involve alterations to a set lifestyle, which in turn affects the relationship. If you have had a very active social life consisting of eating out a great deal, parties and late hours, your nauseated, fatigued and pregnant partner may not consider this fun any longer. Sacrifices have to be made, and if both partners are not in agreement about these, arguments and tension naturally arise. Again, communication and a respect and understanding of the pregnancy will help in resolving these conflicts.

Another change that fathers can expect throughout the pregnancy is a definite lack of attention by friends and relatives. This is especially true with first pregnancies when everyone is excited and wants to shower the woman with attention and advice. This will prepare you for when the baby arrives and neither you nor your partner get any attention.

Hopefully, by the time a couple decides to have a child, they know each other well enough to understand the other's needs and desires. Early pregnancy is a good time to talk about those needs since they will probably require altering in some fashion. If the woman is very sick in the first trimester, she may need her partner to pitch in more around the house, especially with the cooking. This may mean that dinner has to be at a different time to allow the man to prepare the meal after he gets home from work. If you have other children, more help with childcare may be needed. All these things should be spelled out so that resentment doesn't fester through one partner assuming that the other knows what he or she wants.

The father's role in labour and childbirth

Fathers can play a very big part for their partners during labour and the actual birth. However, here again it is important to set ground rules early on to reduce the potential for conflict. Decide at an early stage whether you will be with your partner during her labour and the birth. If you feel that this is something that you could not physically or emotionally do, then she should know early so that she can plan to have another support person with her through the labour and birth. Some men have weak stomachs and just cannot tolerate being there. That is OK as long as it is OK with your partner.

It is also worth keeping in mind the possibility that your partner may not want you there at all. This should not be a reflection of her feelings towards you. It is simply that some women prefer to give birth on their own or with another woman in support. You may be disappointed (or you may be relieved) at hearing this news, but it is important to back up your partner's choice.

If your partner does want your support and you plan to be with her through labour and delivery, discuss with her what she wants you to do. Some women want more hands-on support (e.g. back rubs, foot massage), and other women prefer their partners to be there but not to touch them. It is the father's role during labour to cater to his partner's every whim. Women tend to be very clear about what they want once labour begins, and men should accommodate them. Labour is intensely painful and incredibly hard work, and no woman should have to think twice about receiving the support she needs and wants.

Most men are not fully prepared for the amount of suffering they see their partners experiencing during labour. Sometimes childbirth classes may lead you to believe that if the woman does the breathing exercises, she won't feel any pain. Well, that is not the case by any means, and men should be prepared to see their partners suffering quite a bit. The experience is very different from watching an actress in a film or on television going through labour pains. When it is someone you love very much who is going through all of this while you stand by helplessly, it can be very upsetting indeed. Seeing a loved one in pain is difficult. Understand that this is nature's way, and you can help by giving your partner whatever it is that she wants. That may range from giving her sips of water, to staying up for two nights in a row rubbing her back.

There are several things you should be prepared for during the labour. One is blood. There is almost always a fair amount of blood during labour and delivery, and while you probably won't have to clean it up, you should expect to see it. It is normal. Also, close to delivery, many women vomit. Be prepared for that by finding out where the basin is, in case you are the only one around at the time. In addition, during the pushing stage, your partner will probably move her bowels. This also is very normal, although it may be mortifying to some men — it usually is to the woman. Be assured that those taking care of your partner see this all the time; in fact, it is a good sign that she is making progress. Never, never make a comment about this as it will only add to her embarrassment needlessly. Your partner may cry or even scream during the labour and delivery. When you see how hard she is working, you will understand this, and again, you should never make a derogatory comment about it. Only offer support.

Another decision that should be made ahead of time is about how much the father will actually be able to participate in the birth. Most doctors or midwives will allow the father to cut the umbilical cord if he so desires. Some will even let him deliver the baby once the head and shoulders are out. If you both decide that this is what you want for the birth, talk to your doctor or midwife about it well ahead of time so arrangements can be made and instructions given.

Another important role that fathers have during the birth and soon after is the picture taking. If you both decide that you want to photograph the event, be prepared in advance by making sure that your camera has film in it. An extra roll of film is also a good idea. Remember, too, to take the camera to the hospital if that is where the birth is to take place. It certainly is an event that can't be recaptured, so put the camera in the suitcase early.

Your other children

Some recent research has been done on having children present during the birth of a brother or sister. No long-term conclusive results have been obtained since this is a fairly recent phenomenon, but it is speculated that, like having the father at the birth, other children will feel closer to the baby and sibling rivalry would be reduced. However, while some studies have shown this to be true, others have not.

If you plan to have your baby at home, it is obviously your choice whether to have your other children there or not. Some hospitals and birth centres do allow this as long as there is also someone there (other than the person giving support to the woman) to watch over the children. This "caretaker" must also be ready to take away the child or children immediately if they no longer want to stay.

Usually there is a special class that the children must attend to prepare them for what to expect during labour and childbirth. There are also recommended books on the subject.

Just as fathers get upset about seeing their partners in pain, children likewise are uncomfortable with this. Children should be carefully prepared to see their mothers crying, screaming or vomiting. The blood doesn't seem to bother children as much as seeing their mothers in pain. If you are considering having your children there with you at the birth, talk to your doctor or midwife about what arrangements have to be made ahead of time.

If this is not a first baby, fathers and the brothers and sisters of the new baby have the opportunity to develop a special bond during the pregnancy and in the post-natal period. Since your partner needs more time to rest, you can take the time to nurture your relationship with your other children and give her time to recuperate. Looking at this as a positive experience can make all the difference in the world. Children certainly look forward to special attention from a parent who is usually at work all day.

The mother and newborn will be the centre of attention after the birth, and it is natural for the next oldest child to feel jealous and act badly. This can be stressful on everyone and it is almost always unavoidable, no matter how well you prepare the child. The father can play a big role in smoothing the transition to life with a new baby in the home, and in many instances, this is the first opportunity for Dad to be the sole attention-giver to the child(ren). A good idea is to give a present to each of the other children from the new baby upon his or her arrival at home. This keeps them occupied for a little while and fosters some positive feelings about this new member of the family. Small children respond quite well to concrete rewards, as long as they are not overdone. It is also a good idea to make plans for special outings, not only to keep them occupied, but also to take advantage of this special time alone together. All too soon, the routine of life will exert itself, and your children will return to their usual preoccupations. You can never get that time back again.

Single mothers

It is a fairly common occurrence for a woman to find herself pregnant outside a relationship with a male partner. Sometimes this is a conscious choice, such as deciding to become pregnant by someone you are not involved with, or by insemination, which is becoming more common. Other times, it occurs because of circumstances, as with a separation or divorce during the pregnancy.

If you are not involved in a relationship with one particular person, you needn't feel that you have to go through your pregnancy alone. You should be encouraged to bring a support person with you to childbirth classes, but that person need not be the father of the baby. It may be a close friend (male or female), your mother, your sister or whomever you want. Hospitals also allow you to have someone with you during the labour and the birth, but it doesn't have to be the father. Many women want to have their mothers there or a female friend or relative. Some centres allow you to have two people at the birth. Ask your doctor or midwife what the policy is where you will be having your baby. If you are having your baby at home, you can have whomever and how many you want.

In some cultures, childbirth is strictly a female event and men are not allowed to be there. In Western cultures, this is not the norm, but you should not be criticized if you do not want a man around. Again, this is your body and your child; you have the right to make these decisions on your own. This is as true for women with male partners as it is for single mothers.

If you are alone during the pregnancy because of a sudden break-up, separation, divorce or death, the emotional adjustment may be very difficult. Not only will you have to deal with the painful emotions of loss and grief, but you have the physical discomforts as well. The future plans you dreamed about as a couple have to be changed now that you will be a single parent. This process can be a very painful one. It helps if you have a lot of supportive friends and relatives with whom to share your feelings. Professional counselling may also be helpful in resolving your loss, and it can give you some constructive ways to pull your life together again.

PART III

The Birth

CHAPTER ELEVEN

Labour and Childbirth

We have all heard a multitude of horror stories about labour. Most women love to relate their labour stories, good or bad, for the rest of their lives. Therefore, you will probably be exposed to the range of women's experience – from being knocked out with a general anaesthetic and waking up when the baby is three days old to the totally natural home birth. Most of these stories are laced throughout with the word *pain*. It hurts to have a baby, there is no denying that, but many women approach the event with fear in their hearts. There is fear of the unknown. Is it really as bad as everyone says? Will I be able to stand it? I never was very good with pain: am I capable of going through with this? These are all questions that may run through your mind as your due date approaches. By the time these thoughts, worries, concerns and fears become pronounced, usually between 35 and 39 weeks, there is no going back – the baby has to come out sooner or later. By 39 weeks, you may have become much more uncomfortable, so uncomfortable, in fact, that you start to look forward to a day of pain just to get the pregnancy over with. If you go past your due date, the anticipation of labour pains may seem downright fun. This seems to be nature's way of getting you emotionally ready for some intense physical discomfort.

Preparing for labour

Childbirth classes are now widely available and used by millions of pregnant women and their partners. The basis for this preparation was originated in the Soviet Union, by Dr Ferdinand Lamaze in

1951. His theory was that the pain of labour is intensified by fear and that relaxation would greatly minimize the pain involved in childbirth. Therefore the focus of childbirth classes is to inform women about what to expect during labour and delivery, thereby reducing the fear of the unknown. The classes teach relaxation techniques which will minimize the pain involved in labour and delivery. Your doctor or midwife will have information about the childbirth classes in your area; the National Childbirth Trust (see p. 189 for the address and telephone number) runs classes throughout the country, and the hospital where you are going to have your baby may also have classes. The classes usually begin around your 32nd week of pregnancy and usually last six weeks (one evening a week). Most couples feel very positive about these classes, and enjoy sharing their experiences with others going through the same thing. Single women, and women whose partners are not interested in attending the classes, may still attend by themselves or with a friend or relative of their choice.

The signs of labour

From about 37 weeks, you will begin to wonder when your labour will begin, and what it will be like. There are many signs of labour, some of them subtle, some of them very apparent, not all of them experienced in every pregnancy.

The baby "drops" (lightening)

If this is your first baby, it will usually descend down into your pelvis, usually two but even three to four weeks before you go into labour. For some women this is a very noticeable event. It may happen suddenly or it may occur gradually over a day or two. The most prominent signs of lightening are the increased pressure you feel in your pelvic area, accompanied by an increased need to urinate, and the ability to breathe a little easier. Once the baby drops into your pelvis, it is said to have become "engaged".

For women who have had a baby before, this phenomenon does not usually occur until sometime close to the onset of labour – a few hours or a few days.

Not all women experience lightening, so don't be alarmed if you don't notice these changes.

Energy spurt or "nesting"

During the day before labour starts, women sometimes feel a huge burst of energy and spend several hours shopping, cleaning or getting things ready for the baby. This doesn't happen to everyone, but many women do notice a change in their energy level on that day. If this happens to you, don't overdo it. Most women don't recognize this energy spurt for what it is until labour starts, so in general take it easy towards the end of your pregnancy. Labour takes a lot of stamina, so be sure to have a few rest periods every day.

"Bloody show"

The cervix always has mucus in and around it. In pregnancy, there is usually a thick "plug" of mucus lodged inside the cervical canal which prevents bacteria from ascending into the uterus. As the cervix starts to soften and dilate, this plug is often expelled along with some blood. It may happen a week or two or it may happen an hour or so before labour starts, it may happen mid-way through labour, or it may never happen at all. All of these scenarios are normal. If you do pass your mucus plug, it is not necessary to call your doctor or midwife. Simply keep note of when it occurred, and know that it is normal.

Diarrhoea

You may experience diarrhoea or loose bowel movements a few hours before you start labour. Again, this does not happen with everyone, but it may be a sign of impending labour. It is a normal way of clearing the tract for the baby, and should not be regarded as an illness or abnormality. It is especially noticeable if you've been constipated for some time, but women with normally loose stools may not see any difference.

Nausea and loss of appetite

Some women are repulsed by food just before or at the onset of labour, and most women have lost their appetite by the time they are in the active part of labour. Some women, of course, never lose their appetite at all, and that's normal too, though less common. When labour starts, much of the blood flow is shunted away from the stomach to the uterus to supply nutrients and oxygen for the intense work it will be doing. Whenever blood is shunted away from the stomach, nausea ensues.

Ruptured membranes ("breaking of the waters")

For some women, the onset of labour is marked by their "waters" breaking. It may be a big gush of fluid, or it may be a trickle that continuously leaks out. If your waters break, the most important thing to do is note what colour the fluid is. If the fluid is yellow, green or brown, call your doctor or midwife immediately; the baby may at some point have been stressed and has had a bowel movement (meconium) in the amniotic fluid. Most doctors and midwives will want you to go to hospital immediately so that the baby can be monitored for any signs of foetal distress. If the fluid is clear, and especially if it happens at night, it is usually all right to wait until the morning to call your doctor or midwife, as long as you have no contractions. Ask your doctor or midwife beforehand what she or he prefers. If your waters break, do not put anything into your vagina – no tampons, no fingers and do not have sexual intercourse. Anything inserted into the vagina increases your chance of developing an infection. Place a clean towel between your legs to catch the fluid.

Sometimes at the end of pregnancy, urinary incontinence is mistaken for the rupture of membranes. This can be confusing, especially if the fluid is trickling rather than gushing out. Also, the mucous secretions from the vagina at this time are very watery and may be mistaken for amniotic fluid. If you are unsure, first of all empty your bladder. Then put on a sanitary towel and note the colour of the fluid on the pad and how long it takes the pad to become soaked. If it is indeed amniotic fluid, you will have no control over it, it should have no odour and the pad will be wet continuously.

Most women (88%) go into labour within 48 hours of breaking their waters. It was felt, until recently, that unless you had the baby within 24 hours of breaking your waters, your risk of infection was high. Therefore, many women with ruptured membranes had labour induced in order to be delivered within 24 hours. Recent studies have indicated, however, that if left alone, and without putting anything in the vagina, most women go into labour spontaneously within 48 hours, and the infection rate is lower than in those who were induced. A sterile speculum examination may be done by your doctor or midwife to confirm the ruptured membranes. A hand examination should, however, be avoided.

During one of your antenatal appointments, ask your doctor or midwife what their routine is. The management of ruptured membranes varies widely, and it is best to find out what is considered acceptable by those from whom you receive care. If you do not want to be induced for ruptured membranes, however, discuss with your doctor or midwife the possibility of letting you go into labour spontaneously.

Backache
Some women experience a lower backache either before the onset of labour or through the beginning phase. Since you may have had backache throughout the latter part of pregnancy, you might not consider this significant, until afterwards.

Contractions
These are what every pregnant woman is waiting for. From about 38 weeks, every little twinge will make you stop and say, "Was that one?" "Should I start timing these?" Relax. Almost no one goes through labour without knowing it. If you are not sure if it was a contraction or not, it probably wasn't.

How to tell the difference between real labour and false labour
Contractions usually start out feeling like bad period pains. There is a rhythm to the pattern: they start out mild, gradually build to a peak, then slowly go away. They are like waves of pain. After a while, you'll start to see the pattern. If you put your hand on the top of your belly, you'll feel the uterus tighten as the contraction builds. The pains may be spaced every 30 minutes to start, or they may occur every five minutes. These may be felt primarily in your groin area, or, in the case of back labour, in your lower back. It takes a while to distinguish whether or not this is the real thing. False labour is a common occurrence, and can be differentiated from real labour in the following ways:

● Have something to drink. If you are even slightly dehydrated, you may experience contractions at regular intervals. Often, putting fluids back into your system will be enough to stop the contractions completely.
● Take a warm bath if your waters have not broken. This will relax you and, if it is false labour, will stop the contractions.
● Have a glass of wine. This has the same relaxation effect as a bath, and usually makes the contractions stop if they are not the real thing. The wine and the bath together are a great combination.
● Walk around a little bit. If it is false labour, the contractions

become irregular and decrease in frequency or stop. With real labour, walking usually makes the contractions more intense and regular.

If you try one or all of the above measures and your contractions stop, there is no need to call your doctor or midwife (or your partner for that matter). If the contractions become more intense and regular, it's probably safe to assume you are in *early* labour. During an antenatal appointment, discuss with your doctor or midwife when he or she prefers to be contacted. It is not unreasonable to wait until your contractions are five minutes apart, and you cannot walk or talk through them any more. This may be many hours after the onset of contractions, but you are usually much better off at home if you have had no problems with the pregnancy. Again, don't worry that you won't know when you are in labour. You may not recognize it for a few hours, but after a while you really can't mistake it for anything else.

When to call for help

At the end of pregnancy, there are some symptoms which warrant an immediate call for help. If you experience these, contact your doctor or midwife at once.

● *Lack of foetal movement.* The frequency of the baby's movements decreases right before you go into labour, and that is normal. But you should still feel at least ten kicks a day, or three in an hour after you eat something sweet. If it seems like the baby is moving, but not as much as before, have some sweet juice and lie down on your left side and count the movements. If you feel three movements in the next hour, be reassured. If you don't feel at least three movements, call your doctor or midwife. He or she will most likely want to see you to listen to the baby's heartbeat, and make an assessment.

● *Heavy vaginal bleeding.* If you start to bleed from the vagina as if you were having a menstrual period or even heavier (not just bloody mucus), you should call your doctor or midwife. Note how much blood there is, put absolutely nothing into the vagina, and count the baby's movements. This type of bleeding may be a *placenta praevia* (when the placenta covers the cervix, *see* p. 172), or the placenta may be separating prematurely from the wall of the uterus (*abruptio placenta, see* p. 172). Both complications are serious, and you will need to be evaluated right away.

● *Hard abdomen or one long, sustained contraction.* This may also be a sign of *abruptio placenta*, and may be associated with decreased foetal movement. Again, call immediately.

The stages of labour

The first stage

The first stage of labour is defined as the time during which regular contractions cause your cervix to open up by 10 centimetres (4 inches), when it is called "fully dilated". The cervix needs to be fully dilated for the baby to pass through it. This stage of labour is broken down into three phases: the latent, active and transition phases.

The latent phase

This is the time during which you are contracting, usually mildly, and your cervix opens to about 4 centimetres. This phase may take up to 14 hours with a first baby, and up to 7 or 8 hours with subsequent babies. Usually the contractions are 10 minutes or more apart, and very tolerable. You may not even need to use any breathing techniques during this phase.

During latent labour, you are much better off staying at home if you have no medical problems. You will probably be much more comfortable in your own surroundings, and your labour will progress much better if you are comfortable. You should continue to take in fluids during this phase, and eat lightly if you are hungry, as it may be many hours before your baby is born and there is no need to starve yourself. If you don't feel like eating, of course don't force yourself to, but do keep taking in some liquids.

If your waters have not yet broken, taking a warm bath during this phase will help you to relax, and may make you comfortable enough to sleep in between the contractions. If your waters have broken, then try taking a hot shower. You are better off conserving your energy for what is to come and to rest as much as possible during early labour. If you walk for miles, or do heavy housework, you'll be exhausted by the time hard labour sets in, and the pain will be more difficult to cope with. Don't get too involved with timing every single contraction. They'll keep coming whether you time them or not, and until they get very close together, it doesn't matter that much.

The active phase

This is the time when your cervix actively starts to dilate, usually at the rate of about 1 centimetre an hour for a first baby, and 1.5 centimetres an hour for subsequent babies. This phase will bring you to 7 or 8 centimetres dilation. The contractions are much stronger during

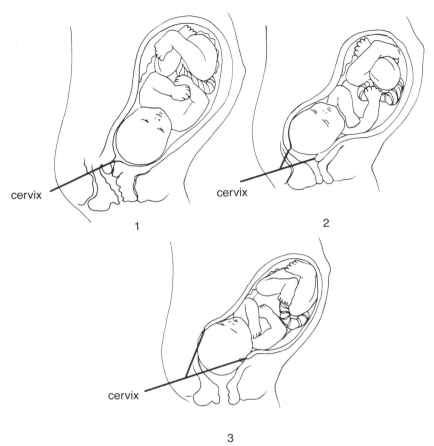

cervix

cervix

1

2

cervix

3

The first stage of labour. (1) The cervix is closed and the baby's head is engaged. (2) The cervix has dilated by about 1 centimetre. (3) The cervix is fully dilated to 10 centimetres (transition).

this period, and you will have to concentrate on relaxing. This is when the breathing techniques learned in childbirth classes become valuable. In fact, even women who have never taken the classes develop their own rhythmic breathing patterns to help them cope with these contractions. The contractions are usually 3 to 5 minutes apart during this phase, so you don't have a long time in between to sleep, but if you can, you should still try to relax to nearly the point of sleep between contractions.

During contractions, you may need to stop what you are doing, stare at a particular spot to concentrate, and do some rhythmic breathing in order to cope with the pain. This is a good time to get back into the bathtub, as the warm water is very relaxing, and relaxation makes the pain more manageable. If your waters have broken, then you should stand in a warm shower rather than sit in a tub of water.

A massage may also be comforting. Be sure to let your partner or support person know what feels goods for you. Some women can't stand to have their belly touched, and some find it soothing.

You should continue to have some clear liquids, such as tea, juice or water, in small sips every so often to keep from becoming dehydrated. Remember, you are doing lots of work.

You will still be able to stay at home through most of this stage if you and your doctor or midwife agree that it is best for you. If you plan on having your baby in hospital, the distance you have to travel will affect that decision, and if you have had a baby before, you probably won't want to stay at home as long as someone having their first baby. (Subsequent labours are usually faster than the first, though equally painful.) This is a personal choice. You should be in the place where you feel most comfortable, and if you are more frightened staying at home, then the place for you is the hospital. Discuss this with your doctor or midwife when you contact him or her. Partners tend to be in a much greater rush to get to hospital than labouring women. If you and your partner disagree about where you should be during your labour, it often helps if your doctor or midwife talks to your partner.

The transition phase
This is the time when your cervix dilates from 7 or 8 centimetres to 10 centimetres and becomes fully dilated. The contractions won't differ a lot from those of the active phase, but they might last a little longer, and they might be a tiny bit less frequent. They do tend to intensify to the peak a little faster, and go away a little more slowly. Every woman is different: some don't notice any change between these contractions and the ones that preceded them, and some women find the transition unbearable.

Some signs of transition include:
• *Nausea and vomiting.* Many women vomit when they have dilated to 7 or 8 centimetres. It is a very common occurrence caused by the

transfer of blood away from the stomach. Don't panic if this happens; it is very normal. It is also unavoidably uncomfortable.

● *Shaking*. You may find that your legs and buttocks shake uncontrollably. This is also very common, and a good sign that things are progressing. It may be a little frightening, but be reassured that it is normal.

● *Lots of "bloody show"*. Some women (but not all) shed a large amount of blood during transition. The cervix bleeds easily as it is dilating, and tends to do so more towards the end. The blood is full of mucus, but it is also bright red and there is much more of it than the early "bloody show". This is also normal, so don't panic, but now is a good time to call your doctor or midwife if you have not already done so.

When is the right time to go to hospital?

Most women get a sense of where they want to be. Having made the choice of having your baby in hospital, at some point during active labour you will probably feel "I don't want to be at home any more. I want to be with someone who knows what they are doing." You may feel frightened, as if your body has gone completely out of control, and you may need some reassurance. If you are no longer comfortable (in the emotional sense) at home, and are no longer reassured by telephone calls to your doctor or midwife, it is probably the right time for you to start heading for hospital. If you are having the above-listed signs of transition, it's also a good idea to think about heading in. If you haven't got a car, or there is no one to drive you, now is the time to ring 999 for an ambulance. Be sure to tell them you are in labour.

If someone does drive you to hospital, it is common to be afraid that your baby will be born in the car. This hardly ever happens, especially with a first baby. It is much more common to get to hospital too early than too late. With a first baby, you can be fully dilated, and still have to push for two or more hours before the baby is born. For subsequent children, the pushing usually lasts an hour or less. Most women want to be in hospital quite a while before they are fully dilated, so don't worry that the baby will pop out in the car. However, if, before you leave for the hospital, you feel pressure in your rectum (as if you need to have a bowel movement), you should call your doctor or midwife right away. It may be the pressure of the baby's head.

143

What to expect in hospital

Hospitals vary widely, as do hospital policies. During your antenatal visits, you should talk in depth with your doctor or midwife about the routines followed by the hospital. Some of the things to ask about include:

- Is monitoring done routinely on every patient?
- What are the indications for internal monitoring? This involves a small clip being attached to the baby's scalp, which gives a continuous record of the baby's heartbeat.
- What is the policy for breaking the waters artificially (*amniotomy*) if they don't break on their own?
- Will you be permitted to walk around if you so desire?
- Will you be allowed to eat or drink anything?
- Will you go through your labour in one room and give birth in another, or will you stay in the same room?

Knowing what to expect when you get to hospital will prevent unpleasant surprises at a time when you are emotionally and physically vulnerable. If you have any concerns at all about specific procedures, ask *before* you go into labour, when you can discuss your options in a reasonable, unharried manner.

The second stage of labour: pushing

The second stage of labour is defined as the time from when the cervix is fully dilated until the birth of the baby. This is when, with the guidance of your midwife or doctor, you will push your baby down through your pelvis into the outside world. Most women are incredibly relieved when they hear that they can start to push, because it means that the end is in sight. You may feel a terrific urge to push, or you may not.

If you do have that urge, you may get a sudden feeling that you are about to have a bowel movement right then. Many, many women worry about moving their bowels when they push. It is mortifying to them to think they will do this with everyone looking on. In fact, most women do move their bowels, and they should. (You should start to prepare yourself for this long before you go into labour.) If you are holding in stool, you are holding in the baby. You can't push and hold at the same time. Be assured that the people taking care of you while you are in labour have dealt with this thousands of times and are much more frustrated when a woman won't push because of her fear of offending them. You will have changeable pads under-

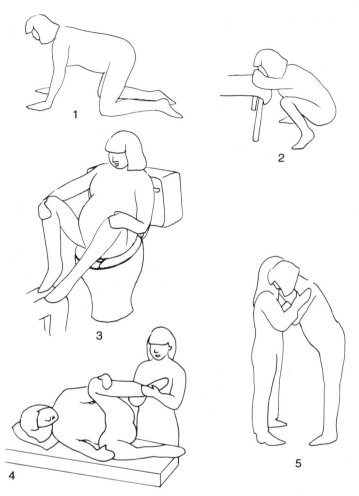

Positions for pushing during the second stage of labour: (1) on hands and knees; (2) squatting; (3) sitting on the toilet; (4) lying on one side; (5) standing.

neath you to catch the blood, mucus and amniotic fluid that will be coming from the vagina during labour, and those pads will catch the stool as well. They are easy to change, and the nurse or midwife will be changing them often to keep you as comfortable as possible.

Pushing can be managed in several different ways and in many different positions. Your midwife or doctor should be evaluating your progress often during this stage, and different positions should

145

be tried if one is not working. For instance, a semi-sitting position is very common, with your knees bent and you grasping and pulling back on them as you push. If you push through several contractions like this and are uncomfortable, and the baby is not coming down with the pushes, you should try a different position. There are several other positions to try out for comfort and ease.

● *Squatting*. Some women love to push in this position, especially if they've squatted a lot during pregnancy. This position opens up the pelvis, and has the benefit of gravity aiding the descent of the baby.

● *Side-lying*. Lying on either side, and curling your body into a "C" with your upper leg supported (either by a support person, or you pulling back on it), is also a good pushing position. This position may help a baby in a posterior position (facing up instead of down) turn its head and progress more easily through the birth canal.

● *Hands and knees*. Getting on to all fours with your shoulders a little bit higher than your hips is another option for pushing. This is also a good way to turn a posterior baby, and may bring some relief for back labour. This position opens up your pelvis, and relaxes your inner thigh muscles. It is a great position to adopt if you find yourself getting very tense when you push.

● *Standing*. If it feels good for you, there is no reason why you can't stand up and push. During a contraction, lean forward on your support person or midwife, stand with your legs apart and push.

● *Sitting on the toilet*. Most women in the Western societies do their best pushing while on the toilet. It is where they most often push for a bowel movement, and here they are not inhibited about moving their bowels during the pushing effort. This works best if you can rest your feet on someone's knees during the contractions.

The birth

As the baby's head gets closer to being delivered, your midwife or doctor will give you very specific instructions, minute by minute, about what to do. At this point, you may have forgotten what you are supposed to be doing, so someone has to tell you every step of the way. Usually, as the head becomes more and more visible – that is, as it "crowns" – you will be instructed to stop pushing so that the head can be eased out slowly, or to give the doctor or midwife time to cut an episiotomy (an incision in the perineum to give the baby's head more room). The pressure of the baby's head is incredibly intense at this point, and it can be very difficult to keep from pushing. You may

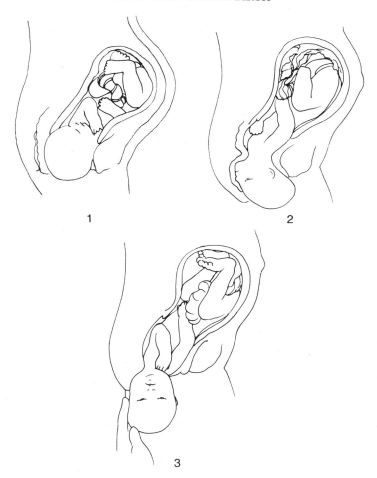

The second stage of labour. (1) The baby's head can be seen and touched. (2) The baby's head has "crowned". (3) The baby's head has been born and the body is quickly following it.

have to blow in short puffs to stop yourself. The advantages of easing the baby out gently and slowly are mostly for your benefit. You will be less likely to tear or need lots of stitches if the head is delivered in a slow, controlled fashion.

You should discuss the topic of episiotomy with your doctor or midwife during your antenatal care, especially if you have strong feelings about it one way or another. Having an episiotomy may

147

shorten the pushing time a little bit, sometimes by as much as half an hour. If there is a problem with the baby's heartbeat, or any other situation that warrants getting the baby out as quickly as possible, an episiotomy is indicated. However, some doctors and midwives, and some hospitals, do them routinely on everyone whether they are needed or not. Some believe that cutting an episiotomy will prevent a tear, and they feel a tear is worse than a clean cut. Recent studies have shown, however, that this theory is unfounded: the worst tears occurred in women whose episiotomies ripped further, and the tears on women without episiotomies were smaller than episiotomies would have been. In short, you don't have to have one; it is possible to deliver a baby without one. Find out the policy of the hospital and/ or your doctor or midwife. If you want to avoid having an episiotomy, have this written into your hospital notes beforehand.

Once the head is delivered, your doctor or midwife will feel to see if the umbilical cord is around the baby's neck. If it is, they will clamp and cut the cord, and then deliver the shoulders. If it is not, you may be asked to give another push to deliver the shoulders and the body slips out easily after that. Some doctors and midwives prefer to wait a few minutes before cutting the cord; others will cut it right away. If you would like them to wait, ask them to do so. Also, if you or your partner would like to cut the cord, that is acceptable in many places. Let your desires be known.

There are different positions in which to deliver the baby, just as there are different positions in which to push. Again, discuss this with those attending you at the birth. Although lying on your back with your legs held apart may be the most comfortable for them and does give them a good view of what is happening, it may not be the most comfortable for you. You can be semi-sitting, squatting, side-lying or on your hands and knees to deliver. Those attending you should be open to alternative positions, so ask ahead of time. Midwives tend to be more comfortable with alternative positions than doctors.

The third stage of labour: delivery of the placenta

The third stage of labour begins with the birth of the baby. After the birth, the dramatic reduction in the size of the uterus causes the placenta (or "afterbirth") to buckle and separate from the uterine wall. This separation is usually helped by further contractions – known as "afterpains" – which are stimulated by your first contact with your baby. By gently pulling on the cord, your doctor or midwife will then deliver the placenta. You may be asked to push a little bit, but don't do so until he or she asks. In some hospitals, a drug is routinely given that makes the uterus contract and deliver the placenta quickly.

This stage can take anywhere from 5 to 30 minutes. If the placenta does not come out within 30 minutes, a manual removal must be done. This involves putting a hand up inside the uterus to remove the placenta. This is very painful, and medication or anaesthesia should be administered before a manual removal is attempted.

Once the placenta is out, the doctor or midwife will examine it to make sure no pieces have broken off and remained in the uterus. They will then examine your vagina and perineum to see if any stitches are needed. If so, an injection of a local anaesthetic will be administered before the stitching is done.

It is very common for you to shake uncontrollably at this time. Your body has just undergone an amazing physical feat and the shaking is in response to that. Having finished the intense work of pushing, you may also suddenly feel cold. The medical staff should provide you with warm blankets as soon as possible.

Pain relief for labour and delivery

It is best to be aware of what painkilling methods are available before you go into labour. Different hospitals have different procedures for pain relief in labour, and you would be wise to ask about these beforehand and remain open to the various options.

The timing of pain relief in labour is very important. Some types given early in labour may stop the labour completely. Sometimes this is just the effect you and your doctor or midwife will want, if you are exhausted and need to sleep before active labour sets in. At other times, however, it merely drags labour out longer than needed.

Pain-relieving drugs given too near the end of labour, close to the time of the birth, may actually cause the baby to become drugged, and therefore not breathe and respond as quickly. All drugs given for pain cross the placenta to the baby. You may see this happening by watching the foetal heart tracing if you have been hooked up to a foetal monitor: there are variations in this tracing when the baby is awake and asleep, and if you are given a pain-relieving drug, the baby's heartbeat will drop a little bit, and will usually go into a sleep pattern. The drugs used during active labour should be short acting so that you and the baby are not affected by them during the birth.

The pain relief most commonly used by women having their babies in hospital is gas-and-air (Entonox), comprising 50 per cent oxygen and 50 per cent nitrous oxide (laughing gas). By inhaling it, the edge is taken off the pain of a contraction while not completely eradicating it, and the woman will feel "high" and perhaps a little dizzy. Gas-and-air is released through a rubber mask by the pushing of a valve; the woman herself has control over the valve so she can take as much or as little of the gas-and-air as she thinks she needs. She inhales just as a contraction begins; the anaesthetic effect builds up and lasts about 60 seconds. Gas-and-air is best during the last (transition) part of the first stage of labour; its effects decrease after about an hour.

There are two types of drugs used during labour: pain relievers and relaxants. The most common pain reliever is pethidine, a powerful narcotic related to morphine. This is injected into the thigh or buttock, the dosage depending on the woman's size. It takes about 10–15 minutes for the woman to feel the effects, but these usually last about two to three hours. It is important to remember that pethidine won't take the pain away completely if you are in active labour. What it will do is take the edge off the peaks of the contractions, and make them more tolerable; it will also help you to relax totally in between contractions and maybe even nod off to sleep.

Pethidine is often given in conjunction with a relaxant, generally the powerful tranquillizer Sparine. This enhances the effects of pethidine and allows you to relax, which alone helps the pain. Sparine is also given by injection, usually in the buttock.

Of course, all of these pain-relief methods can only be used under careful medical supervision, and only when you are in hospital already. If you are having your labour and/or delivery at home, they are not an option. The only thing that may be taken at home (besides a glass or two of wine) is a sleeping pill, prescribed by your doctor or midwife, in very early labour. Never take any medication in labour without specific instructions from your doctor or midwife.

Epidural anaesthesia for labour and delivery

In fairly recent times, a method of partial anaesthesia has become available for women in labour. This is called *epidural anaesthesia*. In

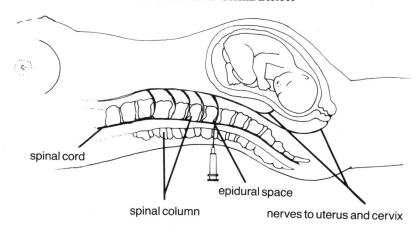

spinal cord

epidural space

spinal column

nerves to uterus and cervix

Epidural anaesthesia blocks the nerve fibres that transmit pain from the uterus. An anaesthetic is injected into the space between the spinal cord and the spinal column, at the point where the nerves to the uterus leave the spine.

this, a local anaesthetic is injected into the epidural space, which is the area between the bony spinal column and the membrane that covers the spinal cord. This allows the woman to move her muscles and allows the uterus to contract while relieving the pain. It can also be used during a Caesarean section (*see* p. 178) if it is not a medical emergency; in this way, the mother can still be awake to welcome her baby.

This form of anaesthesia is not without its risks and side-effects, however. One of the risks is an overdose of the local anaesthetic. If the location of the epidural space in your spine is not detected accurately, there is a risk of injecting the medication into the spinal fluid. Although administration of local anaesthetic into the spinal fluid is done in some medical centres, the dose for this is less than that required for epidural anaesthesia. This obviously would not be done intentionally, and anaesthetists have methods to check that they are in the right spot, but still the risk exists. Another potential risk is a sudden drop in your blood pressure. This could be dangerous for you and the baby and may result in an emergency Caesarean section.

Again, safeguards are used to prevent this happening, one of which is a rapid infusion of fluid by intravenous drip to increase the volume of the mother's blood.

The information given to you about your pain relief options should be discussed with your doctor or midwife, and with the anaesthetist who will be performing the procedure. They should inform you of all the risks and answer all your questions. They would not be doing the procedures if they weren't skilled at them, so don't let the description of the risks terrify you. There are risks to everything, including driving a car, and the benefits must exceed the risks. If your labour is not progressing and you are exhausted and can't bear the pain another minute, pain-relieving drugs or an epidural anaesthesia are safe options.

Developing a birth plan

As your pregnancy progresses, you should start to think about how you would like your labour and delivery to be. Think about your own reactions to the experience, how you react to pain, how you feel about technology and interventions, and how you feel about the creation of a new life. You will receive an ocean of advice and hear more tales than you'll probably want to. All of this takes some time to sort out. Many women start thinking about the birth even before they get pregnant, and those thoughts and feelings shape the decisions they make about such things as whether to have a hospital or a home birth and what type of lifestyle they will have throughout the pregnancy.

Many women write down their thoughts and desires for the birth, and give them to those who are caring for them during their pregnancy. This is called a "birth plan", and you should decide whether it is the right way for you to approach the birth of your child. Most people have some type of birth plan whether they write it down or not. Some just feel more secure if it is in writing; if it is, it can also go into your hospital notes.

Developing a birth plan usually begins with choosing where you will have your baby. This choice is influenced by how you feel about yourself and the care you receive. For instance, a woman who chooses to have a home birth attended by a midwife has already made many choices about the birth. There will be minimal intervention, no medication and no anaesthesia. Conversely, a woman who chooses to go to a major medical centre with the latest in technology and readily available anaesthesia has decided on a completely different alternative.

Once you have made the big decision about how you will be cared for during your pregnancy, labour and childbirth, you will want to find out how different situations are managed in labour and delivery, and what your alternatives are. Again, this is facilitated by having an open honest relationship with your doctor and midwife – decide how you feel about important issues, and then discuss them. The following are some specific areas which should be addressed:

- How do you feel about antenatal testing? What will you do with the results of the tests?
- How do you cope with pain? Will you be open to pain medication if it is needed, or do you want to avoid medication at all costs? What about anaesthesia?
- How involved do you want your partner to be? Can your partner do part of the delivery – such as cutting the cord? Stay with you throughout your time in hospital?
- Will you be allowed to eat while you are in labour?
- How long do you want to stay at home during labour? What does your doctor or midwife think about this?
- How do you feel about your waters being broken artificially?
- Do you want to avoid an episiotomy if possible? Or would you rather have one to make the delivery quicker?
- Are alternative labouring, pushing and delivery positions something you are interested in? What does your doctor/midwife think about them?
- Are your doctor and midwife open to your needs?
- What are your desires in the event of a tragedy during labour and/or birth (i.e stillborn or malformed child)?

These are just some of the things you should think about when planning the birth of your child. If you do not feel your wishes and desires are being respected, perhaps you are with an incompatible caregiver and should find someone else. Different women have different needs, and these should be respected. However, each doctor and midwife has a style and mode of practice that suits him or her. This also needs to be respected, and those caring for you should not be expected to comply with requests with which they feel uncomfortable. It is for this reason that open communication is imperative from the very beginning.

CHAPTER TWELVE

Medical Complications of Pregnancy and Childbirth

When you consider the miracle involved in uniting an egg and a sperm and the formation of a perfect human being, it is understandable that many of these attempted unions will not survive. Luckily, nature can usually identify at an early stage those pregnancies which are not compatible with life.

Early pregnancy loss

Miscarriage
About 12.5–18 per cent of all confirmed pregnancies are lost, or miscarried, in the first 12 weeks. However, more recent information indicates that many, many more pregnancies are lost in the first trimester – perhaps the figure is closer to 75–90 per cent. In many of these cases, the women never even knew they were pregnant; some noticed that their period was a little heavier than usual or that it was a day or two later than expected. Generally, the earlier the miscarriage, the more damaged the baby would have been.

What are the causes of miscarriage? In at least 50–60 per cent of all early pregnancy losses, there is an abnormal combination, or an abnormal amount of genetic material – that is, the wrong number or too many chromosomes.

There are, however, many other things that can cause miscarriages. For instance, the environment in the womb may not be suitable, such as a uterus with structural abnormalities or inadequate hormonal stimulation. In either case, the embryo will not have a lush bed in which to settle and grow. There is also much talk of other factors, including viruses, bacteria and other infective agents; high doses of radiation exposure; severe malnutrition; drug, cigarette and alcohol abuse; and severe chronic disease in the pregnant mother. Environmental factors, particularly if the exposure occurs in the first trimester, can indeed harm the embryo and cause a miscarriage (*see* Chapter 8). However, even extremely potent toxins more readily cause harm to the embryo than cause it to abort. Since the embryo is most susceptible to environmental harm during the first trimester, you should avoid excessive alcohol intake, cigarette smoking or illicit drug use as soon as you plan to get pregnant. However, many causes for miscarriage remain unknown, and most causes remain entirely outside our control. They are nature's way of eliminating those pregnancies which are not healthy and are not destined to thrive.

Because of this, it is not your fault if you have a miscarriage. Even though you may have guilt feelings, it is important to understand that what happened was beyond your control. There will be many people who will try to provide you with reasons for the miscarriage. These may be well-meaning family members, friends or even people with whom you may ordinarily have only superficial contact. The reasons they suggest are usually far-ranging, and can include such everyday activities as lifting bags of shopping, walking up stairs, jogging, cleaning the house, engaging in sports. Just remember that, if these activities did cause early pregnancy loss, the species would not have survived. Other reasons that may be given are emotional stresses such as arguments at home or at work; an accidental fall or slip; a mild blow to the belly by a child; the eating of particular foods or herbs; wearing a tight seatbelt; or having sex.

Despite all the "reasons" offered by others, it is clear that a healthy embryo and foetus are really very strong, and it is the defective ones which are miscarried. Miscarriage is not your fault. Don't allow others to make you feel guilty. You must relinquish any thoughts that you could have controlled the situation or prevented it from occurring. Though it is probably a blessing that this pregnancy has not continued, it does not diminish the sense of loss and grief that occur at the time of the loss. Allow yourself the time and quiet necessary for you, and your partner to grieve. When you have come to terms with what has happened, don't be afraid to try again.

When miscarriage may be imminent

What are the signs and symptoms of miscarriage? The most common symptoms are pain and bleeding. However, in some cases spotting and abdominal cramps are normal, so how will you know when those symptoms are serious?

Some bleeding or staining is common 7–10 days after fertilization. This coincides with the implantation of the embryo, and occurs about the time you would expect your period; because of this, some women do not know that they are pregnant. Bleeding which is as heavy as your normal period is considered abnormal, as is light bleeding which persists for more than three days. In either case, you should call your doctor or midwife immediately. Mild period-like pains or lower abdominal achiness are not uncommon; however, severe cramps or continuous pain warrant a call to your doctor. If the cramping is accompanied by bleeding and/or the passage of pinkish-grey material, this may signify the onset of a miscarriage; again, you should call your doctor immediately. Any material passed should be saved in a container so that it can be examined by your doctor. He or she may choose to send it to a laboratory for further evaluation.

You should be examined to see if your uterus is attempting to expel an unhealthy pregnancy. Ultrasound examination may be helpful in making the diagnosis of miscarriage, but often these events occur too early to be seen on a scan. Sometimes a blood pregnancy test which measures the amount of the pregnancy hormone (*human chorionic gonadotrophin*) may be helpful in distinguishing between a healthy and an unhealthy pregnancy. Very often the examination and the sequence of events that you have reported to your doctor will be sufficient to diagnose a miscarriage.

Types of miscarriage

There are many medical terms which apply to miscarriages. All embryo losses are referred to in medical lingo as "abortions". *Threatened abortions* are characterized by spotting or light bleeding, but on examination, the mouth of the womb (the cervix) remains closed. In *inevitable abortions*, there is usually spotting or slight bleeding, but on examination, the cervix is seen to be open; however, no pregnancy tissue has passed. *Incomplete abortions* are characterized by bleeding and passing of some, but not all, of the pregnancy tissue. *Missed abortions* refer to those pregnancy losses in which the embryo dies but is not passed. In this instance, no bleeding occurs. Missed abortion, also known as a blighted ovum, is a far less common occurrence.

If bleeding has occurred and yet the uterus does not seem to be rejecting the pregnancy, the diagnosis of threatened abortion may be made. On occasion, what may actually be happening is the loss of one twin while the other remains healthy. In these cases, the bleeding stops and the pregnancy matures normally and produces a healthy baby. In other cases of threatened abortion, there is no known cause for the bleeding and the pregnancy proceeds normally. When this has occurred, most doctors recommend decreased activity, no sexual intercourse and sometimes even bedrest. There is no proof that any of these restrictions will improve the ultimate outcome of the pregnancy, but most doctors have no better advice to offer and therefore suggest these limitations in activity. If your pregnancy goes on to miscarry later, at least you will not feel responsible for your pregnancy loss.

If, upon examination, your doctor finds that you have partially miscarried or that you are about to miscarry or that the ovum is blighted and will not develop, he or she may suggest that the uterus be emptied of its non-viable contents by D&C (*dilatation and curettage*). This procedure involves dilating the cervix, if it is not already open, and removing the remaining pregnancy tissue with either suction or a sharp curette. This will effectively stop your bleeding. It will also definitely end a non-viable pregnancy and it will allow you and your partner to start to resolve your feelings of loss.

Repeated miscarriage

If you have had one miscarriage, what are the chances that you will have another one next time? In almost all cases, the chances that your next pregnancy will miscarry are no greater than they were with your first pregnancy. Remember, however, that miscarriage is a common event and that it can occur twice in a row. Successful outcome for a pregnancy following previous miscarriage ranges between 70 and 90 per cent. Repeated spontaneous miscarriages are more likely to be the result of chance than because of any specific cause which will be inevitably repeated over and over again. And even after three spontaneous miscarriages, the viable pregnancy rate ranges between 70 and 85 per cent, no matter what treatment is prescribed.

Late miscarriage

Pregnancy losses after the first trimester affect another 5 per cent of all pregnancies. The most common cause for late pregnancy loss is an incompetent cervix (a cervix which cannot hold a pregnancy inside the uterus). The cervix has usually been injured in some way, either during surgery or because it has previously been opened a number of times artificially (multiple induced dilatations). In addition, women whose mothers took DES (diethyl stilbesterol) an infertility drug used during the 1950s and 1960s, have cervical changes which have been associated with the inability to carry a pregnancy to full term. Unfortunately, the diagnosis of an incompetent cervix can only be made after a pregnancy has been lost in the second trimester.

An incompetent cervix may be corrected in subsequent pregnancies by several different surgical procedures, which are together called *cervical cerclages*. All of them basically involve placing a "purse-string stitch" around the cervix. The stitch is left in place until the baby matures. If you have an incompetent cervix, it is best to avoid strenuous activity.

Ectopic pregnancy

"Ectopic pregnancy" refers to any pregnancy in which the fertilized egg does not implant within the uterus. This includes the most common type of ectopic pregnancy – the tubal pregnancy. About 95 per cent of ectopic pregnancies implant somewhere within one of the Fallopian tubes, the remaining 5 per cent implant elsewhere, in the ovary, anywhere within the abdomen or in the cervix. The incidence of ectopic pregnancy is rapidly rising. For example, the annual incidence in the United States has more than doubled in the past decade, to anywhere between 1 in 250 to 1 in 40 live births.

What is causing this rise? It has been attributed to several factors, including infections which damage and scar the Fallopian tubes, so that the fertilized egg cannot travel down a tube and into the uterus. These infections are caused by sexually transmitted diseases, which have been on the increase for the last 40 years. Infections which follow pregnancies, abortions or miscarriages can also travel through the uterus and up the tubes, causing damage there. If you have had pelvic or abdominal surgery, your tubes may be distorted as a result of post-operative scarring. Other factors which increase the risk of ectopic pregnancy include unsuccessful tubal ligation ("tying the tubes", a sterilization technique) and congenital deformities of the uterus, either caused by the taking of harmful drugs or by rare birth defects. Intrauterine devices – IUDs, i.e. the "coil" – do not cause but have been associated with ectopic pregnancy because they prevent the

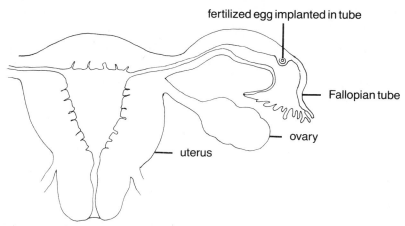

fertilized egg implanted in tube

Fallopian tube

ovary

uterus

A tubal pregnancy — that is, an ectopic pregnancy in one of the Fallopian tubes. Here, there is no space for the embryo to grow and the tube may rupture, which can be life-threatening.

egg from implanting in the uterus, but have no effect in preventing it from implanting elsewhere.

What happens when a pregnancy develops at an abnormal site? A very few of these pregnancies miscarry, just as those in the uterus can. That means that they do not develop but instead degenerate or are expelled from the tube and are eventually absorbed. More commonly, however, ectopic pregnancy can be life-threatening. This occurs when the developing embryo expands and ruptures the Fallopian tube, causing bleeding or haemorrhage. Because of the potentially catastrophic effects, all women, and particularly those who are at risk from ectopic pregnancy, should be well aware of the signs and symptoms of this event.

The signs and symptoms of ectopic pregnancy

The most common symptom is pain, and this may vary greatly in degree. Some women have a sudden sharp pain that comes in spasms, and others complain of a dull, achy pain. Pain is usually on one side of the abdomen or the other but may be more diffuse; it can radiate from side to side or can stay in one spot. Some women have only the sensation of pressure in the rectum. The pain is rarely relieved by anything but may be made worse by coughing or straining. The second most common symptom is bleeding, which can comprise either brown staining or bright red blood.

Signs associated with tubal rupture include sharp, knife-like pain, which becomes dull and radiates around the whole lower abdomen. This is sometimes accompanied by shoulder pain or pain that occurs when the woman takes in a breath. Women also complain of dizziness, weakness or of feeling faint, cold and clammy. These symptoms are common to sudden blood loss or haemorrhage. Although mild pain and cramping are common, you should call your doctor immediately if you feel any of these more serious symptoms.

An ectopic pregnancy requires prompt treatment. This may involve major abdominal surgery to remove the ectopic pregnancy and stop any bleeding. If diagnosed early in its course, it may be possible to remove the abnormally implanted pregnancy (and stop the bleeding) through the laparoscope, an abdominal periscope that is inserted through the belly wall into the abdominal cavity through a 1-centimetre incision just under the belly button.

The loss of any pregnancy can be devastating. But when you go to your doctor expecting reassurance and the pleasure of hearing your baby's heartbeat only to be told that the pregnancy is not healthy, that you may need a surgical procedure or that your own life may also be in danger, the shock and grief are overwhelming. It takes time to heal these emotional wounds. Support groups are available and may be helpful to some couples. Counselling may also be useful in resolving the loss.

Infections in pregnancy

AIDS

Acquired immune deficiency syndrome (AIDS) is the most serious viral infection confronting humanity today. It is caused by the HIV (human immunodeficiency virus), and pregnant women who carry the virus (and who are said to be "HIV-positive") have at least a 40–45 per cent chance of passing it on to their babies. Transmission of the virus can occur any time during pregnancy, and even during the post-natal period through breast milk.

There is no way to test the foetus for the HIV virus before it is born; and after it is born, it carries the mother's HIV marker for about two years, making it difficult to determine whether it is actually infected until that time, unless it becomes ill with full-blown AIDS before the age of two. Those who are HIV-positive are completely healthy; they carry the virus but suffer no ill effects. No one is quite sure what proportion of those who are HIV-positive will go on to develop AIDS; the accepted figure now seems to be well over 50 per cent. Thus far, there is no cure for AIDS.

Chickenpox

If you have been exposed to chickenpox and you are pregnant, don't panic. Many women have had chickenpox as children and are therefore immune. If you can't remember whether you have had this childhood illness, try to find out from your doctor, from your mother or from anyone who would clearly remember. If you have had it, you are immune and you don't have to worry about contracting it again and passing the virus on to your baby.

If you do come down with chickenpox during your pregnancy, the risk of complications to the foetus will depend on which trimester you become ill in. If it is during the first trimester, there is an almost negligible increase in the risk of miscarriage or birth defects. The risk to the baby persists, but at an even lower rate, until 20 weeks, after which there is virtually no risk of any birth defects caused by the chickenpox virus. If you come down with chickenpox within three weeks of childbirth, however, a little less than a quarter of infants will develop the disease. In most cases, chickenpox caught by a newborn from the mother (congenital chickenpox) is a very mild disease. In those rare cases in which the mother comes down with chickenpox within four days of delivery, there is an increased risk that the newborn will be more severely infected and have a more severe case of the disease.

Chlamydia

These organisms are not quite viruses and not quite bacteria, but are grouped in their own family with its own special characteristics. They are sexually transmitted and can live in a woman's cervix, where they can either cause no symptoms or, in a small percentage of cases, they may cause an increased risk of infection leading to premature labour.

The biggest risk posed to the baby is around the time of the birth. During labour and delivery, the foetus can be exposed to the chlamydia organism, which can infect the baby's eyes and lungs. The eye infection can be of such severity that it can cause blindness. If the baby shows signs of "sticky eye" (conjunctivitis) within 4–20 days

161

after birth, he or she is given erythromycin eye drops. If the baby picks up a chlamydial infection in the lungs, he or she can develop severe pneumonia; again, erythromycin is the antibiotic of choice. Since chlamydia can be successfully treated in the mother with the use of antibiotics, the best course of action is to suspect possible infection, take a culture of the cervix, and treat all infections with appropriate antibiotics.

Cytomegalovirus (CMV)

CMV is one of the most common viruses in the population. When tests have been carried out in groups of adults, 40–100 per cent have been shown to have been exposed to this virus. Initial infection with CMV does not usually produce symptoms, but it has been shown recently that anyone who has had CMV in the past can get a reactivation of the virus.

Since so few episodes of the disease result in any symptoms and infection by CMV is so prevalent, it is very difficult to establish any accurate statistics regarding the rate of complications associated with this virus, though they are obviously very low. What is known is that CMV can cause miscarriage or serious damage to the foetal brain and nervous system if the virus passes to the foetus during the first trimester. Unfortunately, whether or not an expectant mother has the virus usually remains unknown because there are no symptoms to cause suspicion, although there is a blood test that will detect the presence of the virus. Therefore, diagnosis of the affected baby usually occurs only after birth. As with all viral illnesses, there is no cure for CMV; the only thing that can be done is to alleviate the symptoms by drinking plenty of fluids and getting rest.

Fifth disease (parvovirus)

B-19 parvovirus causes a disease in children characterized by mild flu-like symptoms and a slightly red rash on the face that resembles a slapped cheek. Outbreaks can occur in small pockets of populations, particularly among schoolchildren. The period when those with this illness are most infectious occurs one or two days prior to the outbreak of the rash, so taking children out of school when the rash develops will not prevent the spread of the disease. Since over half of the adult women who have been tested are already immune to the disease, the risk of infection in pregnant women is thus less than 50 per cent, but the actual number of pregnant women who are exposed to and contract the disease is only about 7 per cent. Only about 10 per cent of that 7 per cent actually pass the virus on to their babies. Of that tiny number of infected foetuses, very few go on to have the rare but severe effects that can lead to miscarriage. Because the statistical chances of foetal harm are so low, it is not recommended that pregnant women avoid contact with school-age children, even when a school outbreak does occur.

Herpes

Genital herpes is one of the most common viruses. Sometimes the initial herpes infection is so subtle that the person who has contracted the virus doesn't even know that he or she has been infected. Therefore it is obvious that, if only those people who know they are herpes carriers are tested for the virus, a large population of silent carriers will be missed. Sometimes the initial herpes infection is more severe and prolonged than subsequent outbreaks; it may consist of a large, exquisitely painful group of blisters in the genital region, and it may be accompanied by fever, joint pains, and a general run-down feeling. During this type of outbreak, the herpes virus is probably travelling through the bloodstream. In pregnancy, the blood-borne virus can be carried across the placenta, where it can affect the foetus. In early pregnancy, it has been thought to increase the chances of miscarriage and birth defects. Later in pregnancy, severe herpes infection has been implicated as a cause for premature labour.

One of the most devastating problems associated with herpes virus infection is if the baby catches the virus at the time of delivery, which can lead to severe neonatal infection (*Herpes simplex neonatorum*). This may result in death of the newborn, or brain damage if the newborn survives. Neonatal infection is actually very rare, although trying to establish accurate statistics is difficult because of the large numbers of people who unknowingly carry the virus.

In the past, it was thought that if women who knew that they carried the virus were screened, with herpes cultures of the cervix and vagina made weekly prior to their delivery, then all those with positive herpes cultures (even if they did not have a visible outbreak of the virus) should undergo a Caesarean section so that the baby would avoid direct contact with the virus in the birth canal. This sounded like a good way to prevent babies contracting neonatal herpes, but in the end, there seemed to be no relationship between the herpes cultures and outbreaks of neonatal herpes. Therefore many

163

women had unnecessary Caesarean sections but the disease was not prevented. Recently, it has been recommended that only those women with active herpes blisters on their genitals should have Caesarean sections. Even if a woman has a history of herpes (or has a partner with a history of herpes) but does not have an active outbreak of the virus at the time of childbirth, she can give birth vaginally with less than a 1 in 1,000 chance of passing the herpes infection on to her newborn.

Listeria

This is a bacterial infection which can cause a wide range of non-specific symptoms such as fever, chills, achiness, headache, backache and malaise. The infection may be so mild and may mimic so many other flu-like illnesses that it will not be diagnosed and you and your doctor will never know you had the disease. Unfortunately, on rare and unpredictable occasions, the bacterium can cross the placenta and infect the newborn. This infection may be mild and go undetected or it may be so severe as to cause premature birth and/or foetal death. If the diagnosis can be made promptly, both the expectant mother and foetus or the infected newborn respond well to penicillin.

Recently listeria has been found in a variety of foods in British supermarkets. As a result, pregnant women are now advised to avoid all soft cheeses (e.g. Brie and Camembert) and pre-packaged dishes (e.g. salads) in the chill cabinet in supermarkets.

Rubella (German measles)

Rubella has become a less common infection since the advent of rubella vaccine in 1969. A more potent vaccine was later developed, which has been in use in the United States since 1979 and since 1988 in the United Kingdom, and most children are now immunized. When rubella does occur in pregnancy, the virus may cross the placenta and infect the foetus. In early pregnancy, this infection confers an increased risk of miscarriage or it may cause a group of severe birth defects (congenital rubella syndrome). About 30 to 35 per cent of infected foetuses who survive exhibit some combination of these birth defects.

Obviously, the best protection for the foetus is an immune mother. It is important that a woman's state of rubella immunity be determined prior to pregnancy. If she is susceptible to the rubella virus, she should be immunized at least three months prior to conception. (In rare cases, even women who have definitely had rubella in the past have lost their immunity, so it is important to check this.) If you have been recently immunized and become pregnant prior to the recommended three months, don't worry – there have been no documented cases of birth defects associated with recent rubella immunization.

Syphilis

This is a sexually transmitted disease caused by the syphilis spirochete. Infection of the foetus with this organism has been a recognized complication of pregnancy since biblical times. If the syphilis spirochete crosses the placenta from an infected mother to her foetus, there is a 40 per cent chance that the baby will die either in the womb or soon after birth. Other infants may be either unaffected or infected with the organism at birth and then develop the symptoms of the infection in the newborn period. Since syphilis can be treated with penicillin and other antibiotics, it is most important that every woman be tested for the infection at the onset and towards the end of her pregnancy. In this way, infected women and their babies can receive proper treatment.

Toxoplasmosis

This is a widespread parasite which can infect all mammals and some birds. Most adults have antibodies to this organism, meaning that they have been exposed to and have successfully fought off toxoplasmosis by the time they have reached adulthood. Because toxoplasmosis is so widespread, some doctors believe that all pregnant women should be routinely tested, but as yet this is not common practice in Britain. It is important to find those women who have a severe toxoplasmosis infection, particularly in their first trimester of pregnancy, because this organism can travel through the mother's bloodstream, cross the placenta and infect the foetus. Although transmission of the infection to the foetus in the first trimester is a rare event, when it does occur it can cause a severe infection that can lead to miscarriage, stillbirth or severe birth defects such as blindness, an excess of fluid in the brain (hydrocephaly) and brain damage. Later in pregnancy, a greater percentage of foetuses may be infected, but the resulting infection is usually very mild and not clinically detectable. However, research in the United States and Holland has shown that 50–90 per cent of infected babies that appear normal at birth become blind in one or both eyes by the time they reach the age of 20. In fact, in the UK there is the potential for more than 20 times more babies to be affected by toxoplasmosis than by rubella.

The two most common sources of toxoplasmosis infection are the eating of raw or highly undercooked meat and contact with the faeces of an infected cat. Therefore during your pregnancy, it is best to avoid dishes which contain raw meat and to ensure that your meat is cooked through, though it need not be well-done. You do not need to get rid of your cat during your pregnancy; simply have someone else change the cat's litter, or wear rubber gloves and avoid breathing in the dust if you must do it yourself; also wear gloves when gardening as your soil may contain cat faeces. If you get scratched by the cat, you will not be infected by the parasite.

Like listeria infections, toxoplasmosis infections can be either so mild or so non-specific, mimicking any flu-like syndrome, that you and your doctor may be totally unaware that you have been infected. Just because your infection was mild does not, however, mean that your baby was not infected; that is one of the difficulties in diagnosing this potentially harmful infection. There is now a simple blood test that can check for infection; if toxoplasmosis is diagnosed, the mother can be given drug treatment, as will the newborn after delivery. Even though this test is not available routinely in the UK, you should still be able to have it if you ask for it. It must be carried out a number of times throughout pregnancy.

Urinary tract infections

Bladder infections are characterized by severe burning when passing urine, the need to urinate frequently, and a feeling of having to pass urine all the time even when the bladder has only a few drops of urine in it. They are very common in women, but because of the changes to the urinary system brought on by pregnancy, they occur even more frequently in pregnant women. This condition may also produce no symptoms; 4–7 per cent of pregnant women have bacteria in their urine without any of the symptoms of an infection.

The importance of bladder infections is greater during pregnancy because pregnant women are at an increased risk of having the bacteria from the bladder travel up to the kidneys causing infection there (*pyelonephritis*). Because kidney infections pose serious risks to the well-being of that essential organ, they must be actively treated.

Better yet, they should be prevented by treating the bacteria which can reside in the bladder before they can infect the kidneys. Most of these bacteria can be destroyed with antibiotics. A sample of urine should be tested to determine which bacterium is living in the bladder so that the appropriate antibiotic can be prescribed.

Vaginitis

Many common vaginal infections can still occur during pregnancy. Although a pregnant woman will have an increased amount of normal vaginal discharge (*leukorrhoea*), symptoms such as itching or highly malodorous discharge indicate that an infection is probably present. Most vaginal infections *can* be properly and safely treated during pregnancy, so don't be afraid to tell your doctor or midwife if you have symptoms of a vaginal infection. He or she will send a culture of your discharge to a laboratory so that the organism which is causing the infection can be properly identified.

Chronic medical conditions

Many women have long-standing medical problems ranging from mild conditions such as eczema to more severe problems such as epilepsy. Most pre-existing medical problems are not so severe as to make pregnancy inadvisable. It is most important that, prior to becoming pregnant, you discuss with your doctor the effects of pregnancy on you medical condition and the effects of that condition on your pregnancy. This allows you to consider possible changes in treatments, which can be geared to your forming baby.

Many chronic conditions improve during pregnancy, many stay the same and some get worse. Which course your medical problem may take usually is unpredictable. If you have discussed your condition with your doctor prior to your pregnancy, you will at least know and be prepared for the possible courses it may take .

Pregnancy-associated complications

Diabetes

In Western societies, pregnant women are more likely to have a raised level of sugar in their blood – a primary symptom of diabetes –

because pregnancy is *diabetogenic*. This means that pregnancy engenders a pattern of protein, carbohydrate and sugar usage (metabolism) that mimics the abnormal usage seen in diabetes. African women, on the other hand, seem to have an even more efficient pattern of metabolism, making them less prone to the diabetes of pregnancy (gestational diabetes). It may have a genetic and/or dietary cause but, as yet, why this cultural difference occurs is not known.

Diabetes can cause multiple problems in pregnancy. In women who already have diabetes and whose blood sugar level has been out of control prior to and in the first trimester of their pregnancy, there is a 6–10 per cent rate of birth defects in the foetus. (Overall, among all pregnant women, including diabetic women, the rate of birth defects averages 3 per cent of pregnancies.) In gestational and pre-existing mild diabetes, the mother's blood sugar is passed across the placenta to the baby. The foetus, who is not diabetic, then secretes adequate insulin, which metabolizes the sugar from the mother and packs it away as fat; in addition, insulin also acts as a growth hormone. That is why babies of diabetic mothers tend to be very large (*macrosomic*). Obviously, large babies have greater difficulties fitting through their mothers' pelvises. This can lead to injuries during birth and an increased risk for delivery by Caesarean section.

In pregnancy-induced diabetes as well as in pre-existing diabetes, the placenta is at risk of being damaged by being bathed by a milieu of high blood sugar. A damaged placenta can age more rapidly and, at the end of the pregnancy, fail to pass on essential nutrients to the foetus. In the past, pregnancies complicated by diabetes more commonly ended in stillbirth. Although this risk still exists, intensive antenatal care with stringent control of the blood sugar level has made this and other fatal complications more rare.

It is clear that the identification of pregnant women affected by diabetes, the careful control of their blood sugar levels and the assiduous testing for the well-being of their babies are all essential. All pregnant women are at some risk of developing diabetes of pregnancy and therefore should be offered a simple blood test to screen for diabetes.

It may be necessary to follow this test with the more time-consuming and specific glucose tolerance test if the original screening test comes back with an abnormal value (*see* Chapter 4). The timing of testing is important. It should be done somewhere between 26 and 28 weeks because, prior to that time, maternal blood sugar values are relatively suppressed and do not reach their maximal values until the third trimester, when they plateau. Some of the 3–5 per cent of women diagnosed as having gestational diabetes will be able to control their blood sugar (glucose) levels by following a strict special diet; others will require insulin injections once or twice a day in order to maintain the tight blood sugar control necessary in pregnancy. The use of pills to control diabetes in not an acceptable form of treatment in pregnancy.

Diabetic mothers are prone to many complications of pregnancy. These include the aforementioned propensity for producing large babies, a greater tendency for developing pregnancy-induced high blood pressure (*see below*) and for having babies whose lung maturity is delayed. This last factor complicates further the potential problem of premature delivery in diabetic women. Pregnancies complicated by diabetes should be carefully followed with regular foetal well-being tests (*see* Chapter 4) during the last trimester.

Pregnancy is a stress that seems to uncover the likelihood for the development of diabetes in women later in their lives. Approximately 60 per cent of those who develop diabetes when they are pregnant will go on to develop the full disease in less than 20 years. In addition, women who have developed diabetes during one pregnancy have a 60 per cent chance of developing the condition in a subsequent pregnancy. For this reason, women who have developed pregnancy-induced diabetes in a previous pregnancy should undergo glucose screening in the first trimester of any subsequent pregnancy, and if that value is normal, they should again be tested between 26 and 28 weeks. All women who have had a history of pregnancy-related diabetes should be especially careful to maintain good nutrition and fitness during their entire lives because obesity, like pregnancy, is another stress which can unmask diabetes. These women should be checked regularly as they get older so that, if the disease should develop later in life, it will be diagnosed early in its course.

Pregnancy-induced hypertension (PIH)

Pregnancy may be a time when high blood pressure (hypertension) is uncovered. This fact is related both to the stress placed on the cardiovascular system by the pregnancy and to the frequent monitoring of blood pressure in pregnant women, which is not usually performed on non-pregnant young women. Many of these women will continue to have high blood pressure after their babies are born and should be closely monitored by their family doctors. During their pregnancies, their blood pressure should be kept in a well-controlled range (just as it should be in the non-pregnant state), and if this is done, the risk of increased complications will be kept to a minimum. These complications include: the development of toxaemia (*see below*); premature ageing of the placenta, which, as in diabetes, can jeopardize the well–being of the foetus as it matures; and premature separation of the placenta (*abruptio placenta*), a rare but catastrophic complication of all hypertensive diseases of pregnancy (*see* pp. 172–74). Because the placenta, the life-sustaining organ of the foetus, ages prematurely when constantly exposed to the stress of high blood pressure, women with high blood pressure during pregnancy should undergo foetal well-being tests (*see* Chapter 4) frequently as their pregnancies progress toward delivery.

Toxaemia

This is a multi-system disease which generally develops during the last trimester of pregnancy and is characterized by raised blood pressure, protein in the urine, swelling (particularly of the hands and face), disturbances of the clotting mechanisms of the body, and a greatly excited nervous system. When, in extreme cases, the central nervous system is in a state of such irritability that it causes the woman to have convulsions ("fits"), the disease is referred to as *eclampsia*; in cases where all of the symptoms except convulsions are present, the disease is referred to as *pre-eclampsia*. More recently, the entire spectrum of this disease has been put under the heading of *pregnancy-induced hypertension* (PIH).

The cause of toxaemia, or PIH, is not known. It is more common in first pregnancies, in women with pre-existing high blood pressure, in those whose mothers had pre-eclampsia, and possibly in those of lower socio-economic backgrounds. Symptoms include sudden weight gain, headache, visual disturbances such as seeing spots in front of the eyes, and dull pain up under the ribs on the right-hand side. Sometimes, in mild cases, the symptoms will disappear if the woman rests in bed on her right or left side.

Since the disease is cured by the birth of the baby, delivery should be planned as soon as the foetus is mature and the cervix is ripe for delivery or, in severe cases, as soon as possible. If the foetus is still very immature, a decision will have to be made after weighing its ability to survive in a neonatal intensive care unit against the threat to its existence in the compromised environment of the pre-eclamptic uterus. Various medications may be tried over the short term so that the woman's condition may be sufficiently stabilized in order for this decision to be made in the least harried circumstances. It must be remembered that the very sustained rise in blood pressure as found in severe toxaemia is a threat to the health of the mother and the baby and can be "cured" only by delivery.

Intrauterine growth retardation (IUGR)

There are many causes for a baby to be born with a lower-than-expected weight for its size. Babies with IUGR are not just small babies; some women have very healthy babies that are constitutionally small. Babies with IUGR, in addition to having very low birth weight, have reduced fat storage and are less able to thrive after birth. IUGR is one of the leading causes of intrauterine foetal death, or stillbirth.

Most of the causes of IUGR are related to conditions which cause long-term damage to the placenta so that it ages prematurely and thus its ability to pass nutrients to the foetus is reduced. Any disease that can affect small blood vessels, with which the placenta is loaded, can lead to IUGR. These include diabetes and pregnancy-induced hypertension (*see above*), smoking and drug and/or alcohol abuse. Sometimes the cause cannot be pinpointed, but if growth of the foetus seems to lag for any reason, women should stop working, should increase left- or right-sided bedrest (which tends to increase blood flow through the placenta) and should be monitored frequently. Monitoring for IUGR includes a series of measurements of the foetus and the amount of amniotic fluid by ultrasound, non-stress tests, stress tests, biophysical profiles (*see* Chapter 4) and certain blood tests. If the amount of amniotic fluid decreases to an ominously low level, or if an ultrasound scan reveals that the foetus is no longer showing signs of good health, or if foetal growth seems to stop, then delivery should be planned as soon as possible.

Excessive amniotic fluid (hydramnios)

The presence of excessive amniotic fluid (formerly called *polyhydramnios* and now referred to as *hydramnios*) can be related to a number of conditions of pregnancy. Two of the most common include diabetes and severe abnormalities of the foetus. If the foetus seems larger than expected for the date of the pregnancy, an ultrasound scan may indeed reveal a large baby or twins or an overly large uterus, (such as one enlarged by a non-cancerous growth such as a fibroid), or it may reveal an excessive amount of amniotic fluid. In this case, if diabetes has been ruled out, careful examination of the foetus should be performed looking for any abnormalities, particularly of the spinal cord or of the spinal fluid and the brain. Sometimes there may be an excessive amount of fluid but the baby is fine; in this case, the cause may never be determined. Excessive amniotic fluid, whatever its cause, can stretch the uterus, making it more prone to premature labour and, after delivery, to post-partum haemorrhage.

Placenta praevia

If the placenta covers the internal opening of the cervix, it is called a *complete or central placenta praevia*. If it only partially covers the internal cervical opening, then it is called a *partial placenta praevia*; and if it lies close to the cervical opening low in the uterus, it is called a *low-lying placenta*. All of these conditions may cause painless vaginal bleeding, in which case an ultrasound scan should be able to ascertain the position of the placenta. Early in pregnancy, the placenta may appear to be low-lying, but late in pregnancy the upper segment of the uterus grows and pulls up the placenta away from the cervix. If, by the last trimester of pregnancy, the placenta is truly covering the cervix, then delivery by Caesarean section must be planned. If spontaneous labour begins, the cervix will start to open, and with the placenta preceding the baby and lying right over the cervix, severe bleeding (haemorrhage) can occur. If this happens, an emergency Caesarean section must be performed.

Abruptio placenta

If the placenta should separate from the uterus prior to the delivery of the baby, this is called a *placental abruption (abruptio placenta)*. This potentially catastrophic event is associated with the hypertensive diseases of pregnancy and IUGR (*see above*) and with cigarette, alcohol and drug abuse. Clearly, if the entire placenta sheers off the wall of the uterus, the baby will lose its source of life-sustaining

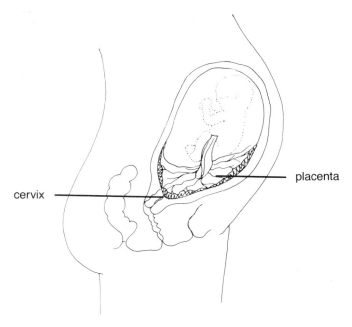

cervix

placenta

Complete placenta praevia. The placenta completely covers the opening to the cervix.

oxygen and nutrients, and if not immediately delivered, it will die. If only part of the placenta separates from the uterus (a *partial abruption*), then the baby will lose a portion of its nutrient-supplying organ and may indicate this loss by becoming noticeably quieter. Sometimes an ultrasound scan can reveal the damaged area of the placenta, and sometimes foetal well-being studies (*see* Chapter 4) will indicate that the baby is living in a compromised environment. If this occurs and the baby is mature, then delivery is indicated. If the baby is immature, then bedrest and intensive monitoring can sometimes be attempted in order to buy enough time for the baby to mature.

If placental abruption is occurring, there will generally be continuous uterine pain, sometimes accompanied by bleeding. If you experience unremitting pain over your entire abdomen with or without vaginal bleeding and/or intense contractions a minute or less apart, accompanied by a decrease or lack of foetal movement, you should

173

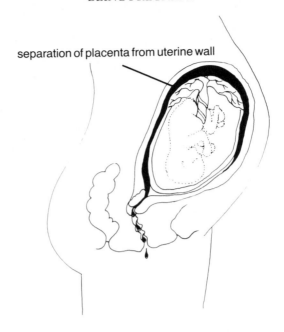

separation of placenta from uterine wall

Abruptio placenta. The placenta is beginning to separate from the uterus wall, and blood can be lost through the vagina.

call your doctor at once. Placental abruption is an obstetric emergency.

Post-dates pregnancy

If your pregnancy goes more than two weeks past your due date (i.e. 42 weeks or more), then your baby is considered to be postmature. Do not think, however, that if you do not deliver by your due date, your baby is in danger. Your due date is calculated as 40 weeks after your last period, and your baby should be expected on that date, give or take two weeks. Most women are sick of being pregnant by 38 weeks, but your baby may not be sick of the environment of your uterus – there, the baby is warm, has a free pool to paddle in and continuous room service. However, as the placenta starts to age, some of these luxuries may begin to diminish, and by 42 weeks there is a risk that placental ageing may jeopardize foetal well–being because of the placenta's inability to supply the necessary nutrients. If you have not delivered by $41\frac{1}{2}$ weeks, your doctor will probably start a regular programme of foetal well-being tests (*see* Chapter 4) in an effort to pinpoint whether the baby's environment is becoming compromised. Since placental "burn-out" will finally occur in all pregnancies, delivery should be planned as soon as your cervix is ripe for delivery if your pregnancy has lasted longer than $41\frac{1}{2}$ weeks; this means that labour may need to be induced. Of course, your due date must be well-documented, with information obtained early in your pregnancy such as known date of conception, early first examination and/or early ultrasound scan.

Multiple births

The number of complicating factors involved in a multiple-birth pregnancy is directly related to the number of babies involved. Obviously, quintuplets pose many more risks than do twins.

Twins occur naturally in a little more than 1 in every 100 pregnancies. Infertility drugs may increase the incidence of multiple births. With Clomid (clomiphene citrate) the incidence of twins may be somewhat increased; whereas Pergonal (menotrophin) increases the chances of conceiving twins, triplets, quadruplets, quintuplets, etc. If *in vitro* fertilization ("test-tube babies") is successful, multiple births are increased because multiple embryos are implanted in the hope that at least one will survive.

Identical twins occur when one fertilized egg divides and, for some unknown reason, becomes two separate embryos, each carrying the exact same genetic material. Fraternal or non-identical twins occur when two eggs are released during one ovulation period and are fertilized by two different sperm; clearly, their genetic material is not the same, no closer than any brother or sister. Multiple births greater than twins generally result from the fertilization of multiple eggs by multiple sperm, each with its own separate genetic information.

The risks posed by multiple pregnancies are generally not related to genetic make-up of the embryos. However, identical twins share the same placenta, and in some cases one twin may steal all of the nutrients from the other twin (twin-to-twin transfusion), causing decreased well-being in both twins. This compromising situation can usually be diagnosed by a series of ultrasound scans performed every two to four weeks. The size of both twins is estimated, so that any wide discrepancies between the two can be discovered. If the sizes of the twins become markedly different, delivery should be planned.

In all multiple-birth pregnancies, the uterus becomes stretched, making it more prone to premature delivery and, after childbirth, to post-partum haemorrhage. In an effort to reduce the risk of the babies being born too soon, if the cervix appears to be ripening prematurely, bedrest on the left and/or right side may be advised. This is done to increase placental blood flow, which, in turn, may delay the onset of labour. If you are carrying more than one foetus, you may need to plan for the eventuality of reducing your workload or stopping altogether late in the second trimester until at least 36 weeks. At that point, the babies will most likely be sufficiently mature that the risks of prematurity – immature lungs (respiratory distress syndrome or RDS), bleeding within the skull (intracranial bleeding), and potentially life-threatening bowel immaturity – will be minimal. Because multiple birth is associated with post-partum haemorrhage, you will be hooked up to an intravenous drip for fluids during labour and for the possible need of blood should a post-partum haemorrhage occur.

Pregnancy over 35

Pregnancy over the age of 35 is not a complication if you are in general good health. If you do become pregnant at a later age (and you must remember that fertility begins to decrease progressively after the age of 30), your risks in pregnancy are only the genetic risks which increase as you get older, and the medical risks that are generally more common in older people. Obviously, such problems as diabetes, varicose veins and high blood pressure are more common to women who are 40 than to women who are 20. Genetic problems such as Down's syndrome begin to become significantly more frequent in babies born to mothers over the age of 35. If you want to know if your baby has been affected by any genetic defects, you can be screened during the first trimester with CVs or in the second trimester with amniocentesis (*see* Chapter 4). In addition, many more mature women than younger ones carry emotional burdens and fears which can complicate their pregnancies and particularly labour, although some older women face impending motherhood enthusiastically. If you are pregnant and over 35, you should concentrate on maintaining your physical and psychological well-being in order to reduce the risks that age might have on your pregnancy.

Complications during labour and delivery

What happens if things don't go as you planned during labour and childbirth? You can't control your labour any more than you could control your pregnancy. Don't cling to all the things you planned so that you feel frustrated or upset if the unexpected occurs. You, your doctor and your midwife share a common goal: a healthy mother and a healthy baby. As disappointed as you may feel if your original birth plan cannot be adhered to, don't feel as if you have failed if what actually happens leads to a healthy baby and mother.

Forceps delivery and vacuum extraction

Sometimes the baby needs some help coming out even though you have managed to push it far down in the birth canal. Sometimes you just don't have any energy left; sometimes epidural anaesthesia, which has given you such good pain relief, interferes with your ability to push effectively; and sometimes the baby develops a problem and needs to be delivered quickly. In these cases, and only if you have already pushed the baby well down into the birth canal, either forceps or a vacuum extractor may be used to help pull the baby as you push.

Forceps come in many varieties, generally named after the obstetrician who designed them, but their differences are subtle. All of them basically resemble large salad spoons; the spoon part of each forcep is slipped into the vagina around the baby's head, the handles are locked together and then pulled on and/or turned. This allows the baby to be manoeuvred into a position from which it can be most easily delivered. By pulling down as you push, the baby can be guided and coaxed down the birth canal.

The vacuum extractor (sometimes called a ventouse) is made of a cup composed of either metal or soft plastic which is placed inside the vagina on the baby's head. The cup is attached by rubber tubing to a suction machine, and this suction allows the doctor to turn and/or pull down on the baby as you push, creating a traction force similar to that of the forceps. Because it takes longer to create the suction required for vacuum extraction than it does to apply the forceps, forceps are usually the tool of choice in emergencies. If the baby cannot be helped out with either forceps or vacuum, a Caesarean section is warranted (*see below*).

Complications associated with forceps deliveries include bruising

177

of the baby's face and/or scalp. Usually this is very mild and disappears in a day or two; however, if the delivery was especially difficult, it may last several days or more than a week. If a very large amount of traction is required, the baby's neck can be stretched, pulling on the nerves that go across the baby's shoulders and down its arms. This can cause injury to those nerves, which usually heals but can be permanent. This occurs only *very* rarely.

With vacuum extraction, the baby always develops a swelling of the scalp which resembles a bun of hair (and is called a "chignon"). This goes down in about a day. However, sometimes there is some bleeding into the chignon, creating a large bruise, which can take several days to weeks to disappear. On rare occasions, the vacuum cup causes superficial abrasions of the scalp.

Complications from either vacuum extraction or forceps delivery are low when carried out by a skilled clinician. The benefits they bring by helping at the birth must outweigh the risk of their complications.

Caesarean section

The indications for Caesarean section are manifold: sometimes a baby can't tolerate the stress of labour; sometimes the baby is too big or positioned wrongly to fit through the pelvis; sometimes the cervix just won't dilate or the uterus won't contract adequately even when coaxed with stimulants, and sometimes the mother may have an illness which won't allow her to tolerate labour.

If a Caesarean has not been planned in advance, the ensuing events can seem harrowing. Suddenly, an army of medical personnel – anaesthetists, nurses, the doctor – seem to descend upon you. You will need an intravenous drip and a urinary catheter (a thin tube inserted up the urethra into the bladder to catch urine), and at least part of your pubic hair will be shaved. You will be asked to sign a consent form. You may feel overwhelmed and out of control. You may not have time to ask all of the questions you would like, and you may feel that you can't do so with a room full of anxious and busy strangers, all working feverishly to save your baby. You may also be dealing with feelings of failure – that everything you had planned is going wrong, and that something must be wrong with you because you can't have a baby "normally" and naturally. You must keep in mind that, in many parts of the world, women do not have the chance to have a Caesarean section. Yes, they do have "natural" childbirth, but often it allows nature to take its full course, which includes death of the baby and the mother. So, as disappointed as you may be in not having experienced a vaginal birth, don't feel guilty or overcome by a sense of failure. Caesarean section can be a life-saving procedure.

Caesarean section is major surgery and is not recommended unless there is a good reason for it. The surgery is done with anaesthesia, either general (where you are asleep) or with epidural anaesthesia (where you are numb from the waist down but can be awake to see and hear your baby when it is born). When the anaesthesia wears off, you will realize that you have had major surgery. Caesarean section involves a long cut through the skin and the tissue beneath and into the abdominal cavity, and a cut into the uterus so that the baby can be delivered. These layers are all closed with dissolvable stitches, and the wound takes several weeks to heal. It may be months though before you feel normal again.

Breech presentation

When a baby lies in the womb with its head up at the top of the uterus and its buttocks or feet down at the cervix, it is called a *breech*. If, during delivery, the buttocks come first with the legs stretched straight up over the shoulders, it is called a *frank breech*. Many doctors will deliver this type of breech presentation vaginally; however, many will not and it is important to discuss this issue with your doctor during your pregnancy. Other breech positions, with either one or both feet coming down first (*single or double footling breeches*), are usually delivered by Caesarean section without even trying vaginal delivery first (a trial of labour). If your doctor has, on examination, felt your baby in a breech position during your pregnancy, and the baby does not turn to the head-down position on its own (and all but 3–4 per cent of full-term babies do), then he or she may opt to turn the baby to a head-down position. This procedure(called a *version*) does not always work, and even if it does, sometimes it may need to be repeated if the baby turns back to a breech position. If a version is successful, it reduces your risk of needing a Caesarean section.

CHAPTER THIRTEEN

After You Have Given Birth

The post-natal period begins the moment the baby is delivered. You will probably feel a surge of emotion like nothing you have ever experienced before. Some women feel it the very second they see, touch and smell their babies, and some feel it a few minutes later, first needing time to catch their breath and take in all that has transpired. The contrast in how you feel physically is remarkable. During the pushing stage, you may have felt as if you couldn't go on another minute, and would sleep for a week once you delivered. Then, with the baby in you arms, your senses sharpen and you feel excited and full of energy.

The hormonal change that takes place in your body after childbirth is incredible. This has many emotional and physical effects, and it is best to be aware of them beforehand. When you think about what your body has just done and will do, the pride and sense of awe you may feel about your accomplishments can be overwhelming. You have created from your own body a new person. You have met the physical and emotional demands of this for the past nine months. You have done an amazing amount of physical work during labour, probably losing at least one night's sleep. You will now lose several more nights' sleep caring for this new person, while producing the milk to nourish him or her. It is truly astounding, and women should take pride and satisfaction in this miracle.

Physical changes

There are major physical adjustments to cope with after childbirth, not all of them pleasant.

Pain between the legs

The most noticeably unpleasant one after a vaginal delivery is the tenderness of the perineal/rectal area. Look at the size of your baby, and you will understand why it is going to take a bit of time before you can sit comfortably again. There is intense pressure on the rectum during birth, and women with haemorrhoids will feel particularly uncomfortable for a few days. Fortunately, once the pressure of the baby is off the blood vessels in that region they will shrink rather rapidly. Use the remedies for haemorrhoids discussed in Chapter 3.

If you have had stitches to repair an episiotomy or a tear, those will also be sore. Ice applied to the perineum right after delivery, and left in place for about 12 hours, will keep the swelling to a minimum. After the ice is removed, warm baths are very soothing and will aid the healing process. You may add salt (approximately 2 tablespoons salt to 4 litres water). After urinating or a bowel movement, try squirting warm water (use a clean washing-up liquid bottle or similar bottle) on to your perineal area to clean it, then pat it dry. The stitches used for repairing any damage to your perineum and vagina will dissolve; they do not need to be removed.

The amount of pain and discomfort arising from stitches varies widely. If you had no tears or only very superficial ones, you may feel fine in a day or two. If you have had a forceps delivery (*see* p. 177), or stitches that go into the deep muscle of the rectum, it may be weeks before you feel comfortable. Your first bowel movement may be a very unpleasant experience if the stool is hard, so load up on fluids, and take a stool softener if you need one. If you have taken a pain medication containing codeine or a similar drug during the post-partum period, you are more likely to need a stool softener or prune juice, as these drugs are very constipating. The discomfort you feel can be very upsetting and may add or lead to some post-natal depression, especially if you had assumed you would feel fine as soon as the baby came out. Know that it is normal to have the discomfort. Being prepared for it will make it easier to cope with.

Recovering from a Caesarean

If you have had a Caesarean section (*see* Chapter 12), you will have the additional discomfort of recovering from major abdominal surgery. This requires a longer recovery period in hospital, and you will need more help at home, as lifting and general moving about will be difficult for the first two weeks or so. The post-natal hormonal change is the same as for a vaginal delivery, and you can expect the same emotional swings. However, these changes of mood may be exaggerated somewhat after a Caesarean because you feel more uncomfortable.

The lochia

After delivering a baby, it takes a while for the uterus to get rid of the lining and return to its normal, non-pregnant size. The blood and uterine lining that pass out are called *lochia*, and may last from four to six weeks. It starts out like a heavy period, becoming heavier when the baby breastfeeds since this stimulates your uterus to contract. When your uterus contracts after delivery (as it must if it is to return to normal size), you will feel small gushes of blood, which are especially apparent during the first few days after delivery. You will have to wear sanitary towels to catch the lochia. Gradually the flow becomes lighter and turns more brown then red. By the end of two weeks, all you will have to do is wear a mini pad. Now, the lochia looks like the bleeding that occurs at the end of a period (brownish) and may be scant, but it is usually still there for a few more weeks.

The first day or two after childbirth, you may gush blood after lying down for several hours. Most often this is the result of blood pooling in the vagina while you were lying down, and it escapes when you stand up. If this happens, clean up and put on a fresh sanitary towel. If the discharge returns to a small-to-moderate amount, then everything is normal. However, there is such a thing as "delayed post-partum haemorrage", which can occur a week or two after delivery. This is manifested by blood which gushes continuously, and it can be a serious complication if not recognized immediately. If you are soaking more than one sanitary towel an hour, contact your doctor or midwife right away. It may be necessary for you to take a drug called ergometrine to make your uterus contract and stop bleeding. Breastfeeding will also help.

The lochia discharge is a normal cleansing and resorative phenomenon, and its odour is normally musty. If it becomes very foul smelling, or greenish in colour and frothy, call your doctor or midwife. This may indicate an infection brewing. Do not put anything up your vagina during the post-natal period. Your cervix may still be open a bit, and anything reaching the uterus puts you at great risk of an infection. For the same reason, it is wise to wait until the lochia has stopped before resuming sexual intercourse.

Breast changes

These are marked and seldom go unnoticed. If you are breastfeeding, you should get started as soon as possible after delivery. The baby's sucking is sometimes stronger than you expected and may make your nipples sore initially, but by nursing frequently during the first three days, you will ensure that your milk comes in optimally. Tips for preventing and treating sore nipples follow in the breastfeeding section.

After $2\frac{1}{2}$–3 days, you will start to feel your breasts getting fuller and firmer and more tender. This resembles premenstrual breast tenderness, but is more exaggerated. Wear a firm, supportive bra as soon as possible after delivery; this will help prevent engorgement (overfilling) of the breasts when the milk comes in. Do this whether you are nursing or not.

Breastfeeding

There are entire books devoted to the subject of breastfeeding. It is a good idea to have one of these books to use for reference, as almost every nursing mother needs some help and encouragement at the beginning.

It was felt at one time that preparing your nipples before birth would prevent sore nipples. Recent studies, however, have shown that it doesn't help much at all. It may get you used to touching your breasts if you were not accustomed to doing so before, but that is about the only benefit. The thing that helps most to prevent sore nipples is to position the baby correctly on your breast. Get into a comfortable position (using pillows if necessary), hold the baby securely, get as much of the nipple as you can into his or her mouth (including the areola, the dark skin around the nipple) and relax. Never let the baby suck on just the very end of your nipple; that is sure to make you sore, and may cause blisters or cracks. When you want to switch breasts or stop nursing, break the suction by putting your finger into the corner of the baby's mouth; then gently ease the nipple out. Never just pull it out.

Breastfeeding is one area where you are sure to get conflicting advice. This can be incredibly frustrating, especially if the baby is having trouble latching on. Some people say that you should wake the baby every three hours to nurse; others say that you should let the baby establish his or her own schedule. Some say that you should start by nursing for three minutes per breast and work up to ten minutes a side; others say that you should let the baby nurse as long as he or she wants right from the start. Some say that you should supplement the baby with glucose and water or just water until your milk comes in; others say that babies don't need this. In fact, it is not uncommon to hear conflicting advice five times in one day from different nurses, midwives and doctors, not to mention family members, friends and even perfect strangers!

What should you do? Since you are feeling so vulnerable as a new mother with a hungry baby, it is best to get as much information before the birth as possible, remembering, of course, to be flexible. Be aware of the basics.

- Nurse often and on demand when the baby is awake.
- Nurse in a comfortable position, changing positions to alter the pressure on your nipples.
- Let you nipples air dry after each feeding. Never use soap or drying agents on your nipples; plain water is fine. Smooth lanolin or vitamin E on your nipples after nursing.
- Get as much of the nipple into the baby's mouth as possible.
- Wear a firm bra soon after childbirth to prevent engorgement.
- Drink lots of fluids while you are breastfeeding to replace the fluids your baby is drinking. It is not necessary to drink any more milk than when you were pregnant. Your body will produce its own milk even if you drink none.
- Relax. Being nervous and upset about breastfeeding can sabotage the experience. Remember, babies won't starve themselves, and if you are well nourished, you can breastfeed successfully.

You know your baby better than anyone else. Make the time to evaluate his or her needs and take the advice you are given with a grain of salt. Develop a good relationship with your doctor and midwife, and be sure that he or she is supportive of breastfeeding. Breast milk is *the* perfect food for infants. It contains factors which build up the baby's immunity to infection, is readily available, and is always the perfect temperature.

Both the National Childbirth Trust and the La Lèche League are organizations that give support to breastfeeding mothers. They have many members and are always available with sound advice and information. If you are having a problem with nursing, or if you are breastfeeding well and would like to offer your support to someone

184

who isn't, get in touch with them. The address for the National Childbirth Trust is on page 189, and the La Lèche League can be reached at Box BM3424, London WC1 6XX. When you are having difficulty getting started, it always helps to talk to someone who has gone through the same thing.

Bottle-feeding

If you choose to bottle-feed your baby, there are a few things to do after delivery so your breasts won't become engorged with milk. First of all, do not stimulate your nipples at all. Even when you are in the shower, make sure that the warm water doesn't run on your breasts for a prolonged period of time. Stimulating your breasts will stimulate milk production. Wear a very firm-fitting bra, and put it on as soon as you can after delivery. The support will help to prevent engorgement.

If you do become engorged, placing ice on your breasts will help reduce the swelling. Put a wet face flannel wrapped around an orange in the freezer. It will freeze in a position that enables you to put it over your breasts like a cup. Heat will make the milk flow, so don't ever use hot packs. If a bra doesn't give you enough support, wrap an elastic bandage around your chest. The support this gives will relieve much of the discomfort. If you do not stimulate your breasts in any way, the milk will dry up in a few days. Take a painkiller such as paracetamol or ibuprofen if you need some pain relief.

Some doctors give women a drug called bromocryptine to dry their milk after childbirth. However, recent studies have shown that this medication is not much more effective than using the above measure, and it can have unpleasant side-effects.

Emotional changes

It is normal to feel a bit let down after the initial "high" wears off after childbirth. This is due to a number of things – the hormonal change that is occurring, the lack of sleep that is now part of your life (*see below*) restrictions on your life that are now becoming a reality – and there may be reasons for your depression that are unknown even to you. Some speculate that women experience grief over the loss of the life inside of them.

The post-natal or baby blues, as they are called, usually set in about four or five days after delivery. You may feel weepy, and cry over even trivial things. You may also feel irritable and impatient. These feelings are all normal, and it helps if you and your partner know this. It may last a week or even two, and if you expect it, you may be able to cope with it a little better. If the depression becomes severe, or if it goes on for three weeks or more, call your doctor or midwife. In some cases, severe post-natal depression needs to be treated with therapy. There is a national organization called the Association for Post-natal Illness which can give you information on how to cope with baby blues and post-natal depression. Contact them at 7 Gowan Avenue, London SW6 6RH, tel: 01–731 4867.

Sleep deprivation

One of the major hurdles to overcome during the post-natal period is the sleep deprivation involved in caring for a newborn. This can be brutal: you may be down to as few as three or four hours of sleep a night at the beginning, and for many that is difficult to cope with. If you have other children, it can be even worse, as often the baby is going to sleep just when everyone else is getting up for the day. However, it *will* get better.

Here are some simple coping methods for getting you through the most stressful times:

• Let your partner help with night-time feeds if you are bottle-feeding. If you are breastfeeding, your partner can wind and rock the baby back to sleep if necessary.

• Babies are often fussy in the evening; after you have fed and changed the baby, go to bed for a few hours and let someone else do the walking and rocking.

• Try not to wake up fully during night feeds. Nurse the baby in a comfortable position in the dark, and don't play with him or her. This will let your baby know that this feeding is solely to have hunger needs met, and is not a social time.

• Rest when the baby sleeps during the day. It is very tempting to run around and get things done, but you will end up tired and irritable later in the evening when the baby is most demanding.

• Stay well nourished. You may find it difficult to find time to cook, so try to plan simple meals that require little preparation.

- Accept others' offers of help.
- Most important, keep your sense of humour. Remember, in the great scheme of things this is a short period in children's lives. All too soon will come the time when you will wish that you could still pick them up and cuddle them to make them stop crying. And as many mothers of teenagers point out, "At least with an infant you know where they are at 1.00 a.m."

Diet

If you are breastfeeding, your post-natal diet should not vary much from the one you ate during your pregnancy. You can continue to take your antenatal vitamins, but these should not be a substitute for a healthy diet. If you are very organized, and have a freezer, make meals ahead of time and freeze them. Plan simple menus, and eat lots of fresh fruit and raw vegetables that need little preparation. Let people cook for you if they offer. Most people enjoy being helpful so don't feel guilty. You can do the same for them when the need arises.

If you are bottle-feeding, you don't need to take in as many calories as when you were pregnant, and if you cut down a bit on refined carbohydrates, you should be able to shed some of the weight you gained. You should maintain your fluid and protein intake, however, as your body has some healing to do.

Don't expect to get down to your pre-pregnancy weight right away. It may take from six to nine months to lose all the extra pounds. This can be very discouraging for women who expect to return to a Size 8 soon after delivery. That is unrealistic so don't be too hard on yourself. If the weight does come off easily (as some women find), that's great, but if you have a more realistic expectation of weight loss, you may avoid feeling depressed about it.

Contraception

You should consider yourself fertile from the very first time you resume sexual intercourse after delivery. If you breastfeed, you may not get a period for some time because your ovulation may be suppressed; however, you shouldn't assume you are fully protected from pregnancy while nursing. Many women do ovulate even though they don't have periods. Talk to your doctor or midwife about the variety of methods available after delivery; if you had your baby in hospital, a specially trained nurse may come to talk to you about this there. Most medical personnel will want you to wait until you stop bleeding before resuming sexual intercourse, to avoid infection.

If you are nursing, you will not be able to use the birth control pill until after the baby is weaned. If you had been using a diaphragm (cap) before, this will need to be refitted in case the shape of your vagina and cervix has changed.

Your post-natal check-up

It takes from four to six weeks for your uterus to go back down to its pre-pregnant size. You may pass lochia for the entire six weeks, or you may stop after three weeks. Both of these scenarios are normal. Six weeks is generally regarded as the outer limit of the post-natal period, and it is for this reason that your doctor will probably want to see you then. Before you are discharged from hospital, or once you and your baby are settled at home, you can make an appointment to see him or her. The six-week post-natal examination involves a discussion to see how you are coping and to deal with any problems or questions you may have, as well as an examination of your breasts, a cervical smear (if one was not done at your first antenatal visit) and a pelvic examination to see that your uterus has gone down to its normal size and to check that the stitches have healed normally. Contraception will also be discussed.

USEFUL ADDRESSES

United Kingdom

National Childbirth Trust
Alexandra House
Oldham Terrace
London W3 6NH

Tel: 01 992 8637

Maternity Alliance
15 Britannia Street
London WC1X 9JP

Tel: 01 837 1265/1273

Women's Health and Reproductive
Rights Information Centre
52 Featherstone Street
London EC1Y 8RT

Tel: 01 251 6332

Australia
Adelaide Women's Community
Health Centre
64 Pennington Terrace
North Adelaide 5006
South Australia

Tel: 08267/5366

Brisbane Women's Health Centre
P.O. Box 248
Woolloogabba
Brisbane
QLD 4102

Tel: 393 1622

Elizabeth Women's Community
Health Centre
Elizabeth Way
Elizabeth 5112

Tel: 252 3711

Health Sharing: Women's Health
Information Service
Information Victoria Centre
318 Little Bourke Street
Melbourne 3000

Liverpool Women's Health Centre
P.O. Box 65
Liverpool
NSW 2170

Women's Health Information
Resource Collective Inc.
P.O. Box 187
653 Nicolson Street
Carlton North 3054
Victoria

INDEX